Across the North Pacific

for

Ann Weatherill

Charles Potts

Illustrated by: Smokey Farris

Slough Press
3009 Normand
College Station, Texas 77845

ISBN 0-941720-99-3

Acknowledgments are gratefully extended to the editors and publishers of the following books and periodicals where some of the poems in *Across the North Pacific* have been previously published:

Brazos River Review, Tom Murphy, College Station, Texas
The Café Review, Steve Luttrell, Portland, Maine
Chiron Review, Michael Hathaway, St. John, Kansas
Image, Seattle Arts Commission, Seattle
Land Escapes 2000, Boyd W. Benson, Washington State University, Pullman
Lost River Mountain, Jim Bodeen, Blue Begonia Press, Yakima
Point No Point, Marie McCaffrey, Seattle
The Southwest Women's Poetry Exchange, Carol Merrill, Corrales, New Mexico
The Temple, Stephen Thomas, Walla Walla
This Is a Pen, Jayne Geldart, Fukuoka, Kyushu, Japan
Thunder Sandwich, Jim Chandler, www.thundersandwich.com

Several of the poems also appeared in a joint publication, *Prophet/Profit*, by Charles Potts and Chris Bodor from Poetnoise Press, Beacon, NY, in 2001.

I am profoundly indebted to and acknowledge the help of professor Ron Takemoto of Whitman College whose courses in Japanese I audited; Dr. H.C. Tien of Lansing, Michgan, whose cook's tour of China enabled me to visit parts unavailable to ordinary tourists; Yamada Hisao, consummate scientist, former director of the National Center for Science and Information systems and retired professor from Todai; Hasegawa Toru of Kurume, our guarantor and dear friend who made the stay in Fukuoka possible; Denis Mair, poet and translator of contemporary Chinese; Sheng Zhi, professor of English at the Middle South University of Technology in Changsha; Ali El-Agra, economics professor at Fukuoka University and coordinator of the International Forum at Brighton College; my language partners, Takahashi Tomoki and Hideko Kuga; Kenji Takahashi; Mikki and Yoroko; Dr. Litke, professor emeritus of linguistics at Walla Walla College.

Slough Press
3009 Normand
College Station, Texas 77845

books by **Charles Potts**

poetry

Slash and Burn with Robert McNealy	2001
Prophet/Profit with Chris Bodor	2001
Nature Lovers	2000
Angio Gram	2000
Little Lord Shiva: The Berkeley Poems, 1968	1999
Lost River Mountain	1999
Fascist Haikus	1999
100 Years in Idaho	1996
The Dictatorship of the Environment	1991
A Rite to the Body	1989
Rocky Mountain Man	1978
Charlie Kiot	1976
The Golden Calf	1975
The Trancemigraçion of Menzu	1973
Waiting in Blood	1973
Blue up the Nile	1972
The Litmus Papers	1969
Little Lord Shiva	1969
Burning Snake	1967
Blues From Thurston County	1966

prose

Loading Las Vegas	1991
Valga Krusa	1977
The Opium Must Go Thru	1976

political and economic geography

How the South Finally Won the Civil War: And Controls the Political Future of the United States	1995

Across the North Pacific

Tabling the Contents

The Middle Kingdom

Warmups

Brief Introduction

Language and behavior are two phases of the same phenomena. Speak and do. Talk and act. As we speak so shall we do. We talk about what we've done, what we're doing or are about to do. Without which speech, doing would not be possible.

Across the North Pacific is a prosimetrum examination of the relationship between language and behavior. Pertinent elements of the historic and economic record amassed by the speakers of the three large contending language groups and cultures of the North Pacific Quadrant are brought into play as required: English and American; Japanese; Mandarin Chinese.

The urgency of this work became apparent to me when I realized that the questions that might save English speaking civilization can't even be asked in English. Language is only a moderately effective device for communicating behavior. It is very effective at screening out phenomena it doesn't want to consider, phenomena whose effective grasp could have survival value, as denial is the response of choice when phenomena overwhelms understanding.

The retreat to fantasies is frequently fatal. Psychology is the least understood and most likely realm for finding answers. This original work in linguistic geography may initially baffle, irritate and confuse. I chose to believe that many enlightened men and women will consider the material with an open mind and be stimulated by it. We were promised paradise and are being handed ashes.

The Revelations of "The Chill at Appomattox"—Revised

I had a tremendous breakthrough, coming in a dream last night, possibly the results of looking into the Komantcia [Comanche] one more time. Komantcia is a Uto-Aztecan language. The word both describes and refers to people who love to fight.

Stated metaphorically as a vision it is:

$$D/S \times SOV/SVO = DV$$

To read this as a process, the Dynamism divided by the Stasis or static, times the results of having divided the two syntactical types, equals or leads to a dynamic verb. It may take years to demonstrate the significance of this.

While English has had the dynamic capacity to become the language of freedom and to superbly locate activity in time, the compass has been boxed, or rather the speakers of English have boxed their own compass—this is a sphere we live on after all—and time now works against the speakers of English, captured by the objects of their enterprise, that is they spend too much time protecting the results of their material culture.

The questions that might save English speaking culture can't even be put into or asked in English. If or when they are being asked, the so-called answers are deliberately misleading. So too the cultural problems besetting the other two superficially mono-lingual cultures about to be considered in this narrative, China and Japan. Cultural problems are language problems, created at the level of a particular language.

Einstein: Problems cannot be solved at the same level they are created.

Hofstadter on Calhoun: A static solution to a dynamic situation.

Veblen: The constant predatory reversion of the leisure class, ie got to hang on, to what you've got.

Got is the O in the SVO and created the DOD, the excessive parts. In a perfectly run military civilization, expenditures should be equal only to actual defense requirements. The proportion by which they exceed them, will lead eventually as it did in Rome, to the exhaustion of the hinterland's interest and capacity to support the enterprise.

Speakers of English are more excited about the O—the last item in syntax draws proportionally the most attention.

Speakers of *Nihongo* [Japanese] get more excited about the V, the last item in their syntax, the HOW of what they did to get whatever it is they got.

Process is dynamic; products are static. Superior products are tools of the new electronolithic. Any culture imagining they are the end stasis run an unnecessarily enormous risk and will be reduced to slavery.

Toynbee: Variations of a fallacy are all equally fallacious but they are not all equally preposterous.

The last time the United States produced as a unit was just prior to the knockout blow and neo-Confederate Victory at the end of WWII when the US became the diplomatic as well as the strong arm of the remainder of the British Empire.

This dynamism activated by common defense erased the diffusion in the unequal distribution of O and stimulated cohesive attention on V.

It lapsed immediately back into Staticism with the production of goods sufficient in volume to fund a perpetual military, a state of siege requiring continuous defense, and an economy based on consumerism and expanding export markets, rather than on savings and investment. This two-faced and ultimately totally counter-productive policy has not been divagated from in the ensuing fifty plus years. Speculation is only good for successful speculators while it destroys the general culture.

The reversion to predatory predilections of the speakers of Confederate English is forcing a static solution on a dynamic situation as if they were trying to stuff a living body back into a skeleton.

16

The New York mercantile model and its handmaidens in the industrial Northeast and Midwest get no attention in this paean to power precisely because their preoccupation with O only produces the taxing stream sufficient to bankroll the Confederate drivers. They do not make policy; they fund it, or rather see to it that the uncompensated value added of the working class is siphoned off to fund it leaving their dividends intact and on a growth curve.

Cohesive attention on V is cultural first cause for speakers of Nihongo. They are primarily focused on the process and have a culture quite void of philosophy and theory.

The Vs by which (sometimes called the way or how) they get their Os is where their attention is focused. Note I could have written that: where they focus their attention. How the Dao—not the industrial average DOW—became the way.

To describe their macro behavior in English and give it any heft it is necessary and possible with the flexibility of English syntax, to alter the spatial and temporal position where dynamism can be rendered. I Japanesalize.

It is related to why Spengler would announce that history (or virtually anything else) is best learned as a branch of epistemology.

To epistemologize in the infinitive form contains the verb how.

History learned epistemologically can be rendered poetically where the availability of the learning remains.

The history of the future as literature, where radical syntax (a war of words!) can breakthrough to dynamism in a culture where free speech is actually practiced.

In other words, the English language, contains a way out of the static trap the southern speculators have trapped it in through their remote control of the broadcast media.

Whether it wins or not will depend on the degree of freedom and the freedom for the vectors the speech is allowed.

The revolutionary process, necessary for the speakers of English to avoid slavery, will reinvest the assets that the neo-Confederate leisure class, the new plantation overlords, since the conclusion of WWII, have siphoned off and squirreled away.

The conclusions of the Chill are poised in the fulcrum of the new learning I have to do for the ultimate work. I have a plan although it may be more than a single person can finish.

Morphology and Syntax Since the Deglaciation

I will check   SVO-SOV dynamic of a dozen languages:
English
Nihongo
Komantcia
Nahuatl
Español
Zhong Guo Hua
Lakota
Linear A & B
Jibaru
Sanskrit
Prakit
Tamil

And others as time materializes.

Read all of Korsybski.
Make paradigms of Bandler's SOM [slight of mouth] patterns.
Note how personal imperatives are VO (S merged with V).
Putting the V on the front of the bus is also dynamic.
Korsybski's books and theories will be absorbed. (read).
Edward Sapier will be looked into.
Look into Edward Sapier.
A string of imperatives is a feedback loop.
I may have SOV material for Komantcia in Sven Lilejblad's work on Shoshoni.

To keep this from being an endless temporal sink—Why do I care?

Do the necessary or nothing at all.—Spengler
For me, it is necessary to understand.

[*The Chill at Appomattox,* was the title *How the South Finally Won the Civil War* was initially written under with *How the South...*being the subtitle. Then the book acquired its string theory subtitle: *And Controls the Political Future of the United States.* This is a description of what the book is about, how it operates and why it matters. The new work is an essay in freedom and extraction.]

1994
Revised, July 10th - August 9th, Nagasaki Day, 1999

The Prolog

Language and behavior are two phases of the same phenomenon. The purpose of language is disambiguation. Language is an agreement among native speakers to misrepresent phenomenology until the members of a language group walk sideways off the face of the earth holding hands.

Behavior is controlled by belief. Belief is accessed through language. Without belief there is no behavior. Without language there is no belief. Language and behavior are the twin hazy phases of one phenomenon, the ultimate codependent relationship. You behave as you believe. You believe as you say you do. You say your behavior back to yourself as you act it out. Language is the sound belief gives off when it is acted on and out. There is no behavior independent of belief. There is no consistent behavior inconsistent with belief.

Beliefs reveal themselves in metaphors. *Across the North Pacific*, a history of the future, will make social and political extrapolations from the linguistic and geographical basis of the relationship between the speakers of Mandarin and the speakers of English with a side bet on the speakers of Japanese. *ANP* will be organized around three principal metaphors: "The Open Range" pertains to the English speaking empire whose power base is the middle reaches of North America, centered in Texas; "The Closed Sea" surrounds Japan; "The Middle Kingdom" is in the early growth and expansion phase of a typically 270-300 year dynastic cycle. *ANP* will record the clash of metaphors, the language wars, revealed by belief and expressed in language.

Everyone on earth speaks a variation of the same language. The business of children is to learn the variation used by their caregivers to disambiguate the next second. The more thoroughly children acquire their native language, and the non-native languages of others, the less likely they are to be taken in by misrepresentations of phenomenology and the greater flexibility their behavior will demonstrate. Flexibility has survival value.

In macro-social terms, everybody is doing the same thing. Individual people need eight hours of sleep at least per day. Adequate nutrition, potable water, the affection of others, a matrix for cooperation, protection from severe elements and a ready wit are required. We eat, sleep, make love and war and amuse ourselves to a remarkably familiar degree, although we do it with a wide variety of styles. It is this stylistic difference to which the variations in languages applies and which has coefficient survival value components.

Economic history, the kind that determines political history, is driven by the desire to have lunch. The questions to be resolved in everyone's economic future are: who's buying lunch; what will it consist of; to what degree can I rely upon it?

War is the attempt to control the economic future by force. There are more ways to apply force than are contained in all the lexicographies. Traditional ballistic blood and guts warfare, while not entirely passé, has filled history books with bodies of bad strategy. The war and struggle for control of the Pacific Basin economy between the speakers of Mandarin and the speakers of English has already employed many different forms and before it is resolved will demonstrate many more. This struggle is at least 200 years old and its most intense phases are still before us.

Old famous flashpoints in the struggle include the Opium Wars of the mid-nineteenth century, the Boxer Rebellion and the Maoist triumph of ridding China of foreign domination. First the invading Japanese had to go with American help in WWII, and then the meddling Americans with their support of the Kuomintang during the final phase of the civil war.

The history of Japan is an elaboration of the relationship between people and fish. Japanese economic aggression in China ultimately stimulated the speakers of English to bomb them atomicly rather than risk American blood taking control of their islands by traditional force, similar to the way it was apparently necessary to bludgeon their way across Saipan and Iwo Jima. During this phase, the speakers of Mandarin and the speakers of English were united against the upstart Japanese.

When Metaphors Collide

Begin with a preamble and then go to the three cornered isosceles unfoldment in the following order

The Open Range

The Closed Sea

The Middle Kingdom

Aprés le deluge, c'est moi, as the good frank king reversed himself. Here goes the re-assessment once all the backgrounding and milieu patterning have been made conscious and apparent.

Conclusion: To be sussed out at will

The Open Range

Here be the rip tide of American exuberance after Cornwall threw in the sponge at Yorktown. The grounding of the British claim to an open sea to carte blanche against the Komantia and the remaining natives in a 75 year sweep to San Francisco. Time out for the Civil War. The Texas surge north and the Custer mop up, with nobody left at hand to kill or maim the Roosevelt attentions on Cuba, The Philippine Islands, Puerto Rico, and the remainders of the Spanish Empire. (There is a nice subset to be embedded here about the continuous brawling between the speakers of Spanish and the speakers of English in North America. They will get over it just about the moment it becomes no longer possible to avoid the consequences of the Southern screw up with China and they have to get along to defend the place or else practice their surrender speech in Spanish. They will be so fucked up together by that point that it won't matter who was who. The cross culturization of especially Mexicans and Americans in notably Texas, California and Washington states is barreling ahead).

One hundred years of America as a Pacific Sea power, The Battle of the Coral Sea, the Battle of Midway, the MacArthur occupation of Japan, and the Korean War (Conflict to you bub) where the size of the MK is once again made manifest, not to mention the comic colonial loss of Viet Nam.

The Closed Sea

The world as seen through Japanese eyes, whose fishing grounds were parceled out since Tokugawa *Jidai* and the incredible need they have for an Open Sea, stranded as they are resourceless at the mercy of larger neighbors.

The Middle Kingdom

All history and happenstance.

Homage to DeVoto

Homage to DeVoto: Across the Wide Pacific

This actually has some amusing benefits in that it could be considered from a Chinese or Japanese point of view as easily as by anyone in the Western Hemisphere. It connects me indirectly with Bernard DeVoto [*Across the Wide Missouri*] who may still have some caché in the dwindling intellect of America. It is not time bound as the two former titles were. Now that the title is settled on, fling it back on the front.

> Raid David Deal's mind for the best books on the English in China.
> Find the best book on the Chinese "Pulsation."
> Put in a Neuro Linguistic Programming sidebar.
> Refresh my memory of Chad Hansen.
> Query Alfred Bloom again.
> Get a grip on the H G Wells Book, *The Shape of Things to Come*.
> Review the histories of the future into which this book will fall.
> Write a compelling evidence hook, ie
>> why would anyone want to know this?
> Find the two most intriguing aspects of Sun Tzu.

I used to plan on waiting about ten years before I wrote this to give me a more leisurely run at some of the currently missing components, but the heart attack has accelerated my table. I used to call this book, *A Short History of the 21st Century* and later *A Short History of the Next 100 Years*. There is something to be said for both titles and neither one is quite right. Both appear to confine the insight into a hundred year period and that will not be the case. I want the insight to reverberate indefinitely, continue expanding like the universe itself. The implications of how language, as the talking phase of behavior, actually controls that behavior, are what will radiate into the potential future. I call this linguistic geography.

This book needs to be clean, short and enticingly drawn. I need to make some brief reviews of the history as it has revealed itself so far. I can brush up rather quickly on the Japanese invasions of China after Toyotomi Hideoyoshi unification and incursions thru Korea prefiguring his forces' loss at the Battle of Sekigahara to Tokugawa Iyasu and the commencement of Tokugawa *Jidai*.

The American component is almost exactly 100 years old with the Spanish American War and Roosevelt's ordering of Dewey to take Manila as an undersecretary of the Navy! America's good political instincts of isolating itself from these troubles are perpetually overridden by the capitalist imperative to develop expanding markets, the seesaw baloney of foreign policy, which got globalized with the NSC and the CIA and the Universal State. Find the equivalent of the audit of the energy required to conduct the Pacific War from the American side.

My theory concerns the relationship between language and behavior rather than the intellectual sandtrap of language and thinking. A buttress for my theory is that the CIA was not concocted to go about discovering what the enemies of Truman's state were "thinking" but rather what they were "doing." There is very little evidence of thought anywhere—Voltaire, Heraclitus, Neitzsche, that about covers it, —let alone in the daily behavior of ordinary people slogging it out with their limited grasp of situations, *Across the North Pacific.*

I dug out **Chad Hansen's Monographs** and began to soar again.

I have to renew my acquaintance with the half dozen
Tongs of relevance in the Chinese angle.

Hansen's pragmatics v syntax matrix expostulating concrete sequentialism.
Bloom's If Would.
The rigidity of morphological addition.
The pulsation of the dynastic divergence.
The Meng Tzuian overview of the "complexity and extent of our natural
feelings...sufficient to order the entire world...natural growth model...to
explain thee *xin's* infinite potential...Language has mainly a negative role
in Mencious's theory as the source of distortion, stunting, warping, etc. of
the natural impulses to behavior."

Hansen p 324. "Classical Chinese Philosophy as Linguistic Analysis"

The warm goofy humanism of the contemporary poets.

Ed Dorn's notion that literacy enables you to predict which side to be on,
which means you are pre-dicted before anything happens. Real literacy
might get you to avoid choosing sides. Being literate in many languages
that is, so that perspective, see below, is not distorted by monolinguism.

Patch all of this through the blender of McLuhan, Bandler, Perls, Doi,
Morgan and from the High Level Equilibrium Trap to Mao Zedong's
imperative.

Distort, stunt, warp of Meng Tzu.
Distortion, generalization, deletion of Chomsky.
Language distorts behavior at the transformational or basic level.

Language and behavior are two phases of the same phenomenon.
Which is distorting what in this infinite web of feedback loops?
We are what we speak.
You can't do anything until you've "thought" about it.
You are left speechless.
What is the relationship between speech and language?

The evidence for thought in all languages is too thin and inconclusive.
Nobody knows what they are doing when they claim to be thinking.
Although many claim to and further claim to be capable of deep thought.
There is deep behavior, the kind that gets you into and out of trouble.
Since such actions are frequently taken in utter ignorance of the contesting
parties position, resources or intentions, how could it be said to be the
result of thought?

Situations produce reactions.
Perspective ought to show the superior position.
Good intentions are superior to good positions.
The biological imperative is learning, a natural intention.
Instincts, if they could be identified before they trap you, shorten every
circuit.

How Long Is a Dynasty and When Do We Get Ours?

The first forty years of the American Republic, from 1788 to 1828, have been referred to as the Virginia Dynasty, since all presidents except the Adamses were slave holders from the state of Virginia, as if the word Dynasty could confer some majestic heft on what in retrospect was a very short period. Reference is made in the *Encyclopedia Britannica* to a drought during the reign of Ti-shin, last ruler of the Shang *Chao* or Dynasty as: "Doubtless also the house had lost its power to govern; after about 270 years in the same locale (*about average for a long-lived dynasty*) [my italics—their parenthesis] its line may have well become effete and its bureaucracy inefficient and corrupt."

In average length for a single long-lived dynasty, the entire American Republic still has a ways to go. Long Live the Dynasty! we haven't even had yet. While American history in the long view has to begin with its origins in Ugaritic as it passed from Hittite and Hurrian and on through Greek, Roman, and English history to its present manifestation. Not so many people think of it that way. What to make of 5,000 years of jumping up and down in the same place? What to make of the Chinese history and culture which has had several major dynasties just since the 423 year combined Han *Chao* which straddled the currently used calendar for 200 years on either side of the birth of Christ?

The T'ang, the Sung, the Ming and the Qing, to mention four of the major phases of this length brings us to 1912 and the 37 years of civil war (1912-1949), strife, the Japanese invasion, WWII, which period ended with the Maoist triumph in 1949, "to rid China of foreign domination," and the commencement of the Mao Dynasty.

1949-2222 was a period of 273 years during which China reestablished itself as the Middle Kingdom. A hundred years into the Mao Dynasty, the remaining energy of the middle east and the Middle East itself, came under Chinese suzerainty. There was no obeisance paid to the High Level Equilibrium Trap which stimulated China's retreat from the Indian Ocean in the early Ming *Chao*. With China controlling the energy supply to Korea and Japan, the English speaking Empire of America was deprived of its two most important remaining Asian military bases. The English speakers retreated to Australia, and all of Indonesia was a Chinese zone as well. Africa maintained its charming irrelevance to world history, except as a source of materials, raw and human, as China effectively controlled 70 percent of the world's population, its largest land mass, and a preponderance of world trade.

This set the stage for the Chinese plan to neutralize the Western Hemisphere, except as a place to colonize, which began in Canada in the waning days of the 20th century.

Holy War

Yesterday I went to the trouble of typing into Word the poem, *Blues From Thurston County*, written in late March-early April, 1966, in Olympia, Washington, at the Governor's Hotel, right after my return from Mexico. While it is obviously the work of a 22-year old, there are several places where the language is ecstatic and clear, and treatment aside, it is amazing how consistent my concerns have remained. There is for resonance, the astonishing couplet, "Do you want a / holy war with China?"

The colonial war against Viet Nam was frequently rationalized in the middle sixties as being necessary to contain the spread of Communism, specifically the influence of "Red" China, under the infamous and nonsensical "Domino Theory." It may be a little difficult for people beyond the literate (and they were a tiny minority) of the generations who went through that period to realize what an Orwellian soup the language of public discourse was boiled in.

The pertinence of this couplet to my present work is simply that after twenty-five years of looking, I did in fact discover that the military was the state religion in the Empire of the United States, that all war from their perspective, was holy. After the initial leap across the Pacific which is just now one hundred years old, the Empire of the United States, fronting for the Transnational Corporate Culture centered in New York, London, and Tokyo, is still trying to expand its influence beyond the periphery, where it has been confined since the Maoist triumph in 1949.

The struggle with China for control of the Pacific Basin Economy, the focus of my present work, linguistically based, has been going on for a long time, and oddly enough in some of the same terms. The British who made a fortune addicting Chinese to opium, have been followed by Americans, who are making fortunes addicting Chinese to nicotine.

Well this is not the place to elaborate anything more than the bemused response I had to running across that line in my old poem. I heard another echo in a new poem entitled "bring me the head of saint ishmael" by Mark Hartenbach of East Liverpool, Ohio, which poems finds "something holy in confusion / something i can't find anywhere else." Hartenbach's poem also contains the line "where we can witness total collapse of the cool." The aforementioned *Blues From Thurston County* commences its 4th section with, "Consider / at your leisure / the collapse of cool." Waves come in lengths; that's how they get here.

The Americans, like the Mohammedians whom they most closely resemble, are so intolerantly convinced of the righteousness of their approach, they are insistent on expanding it. The Christian-Capitalist quarrel with Islamic Fundamentalism is a house quarrel. They are functionally indistinguishable one from the other. Certainty leads to violence.

The Americans and their partners in this crime, the Japanese under *Juminto*, the misnamed Liberal-Democratic Party, have majorities of their respective populations convinced that they are living in democracies. The laughter goes on all night.

Magna Carta

The charter of liberties touching the forest.
Prepare for Wapentake
The touching of the lances
Weapon Talk
No amercements will be levied.
Fine.

Men who live outside the forest.
Neither the king nor any of his officers
Shall take another's wood.
No sheriff or any other royal officer
Shall take any free man's horses.

There is so much explosive material it's a wonder that
The king had ever been brought to agree
To the sealing of such a document at all
In which every generation could see its own protection.

English Kings are not famous for their perspicacity.

In 1868, the 14th Amendment to the
American Constitution,
Could trace its ancestry to the *Magna Carta*.

Set this all upon
The Twelve Tables of ancient Rome.

It is *Magna Carta* and its centuries of history
That have made the word inseparable
From the language of freedom.

The drama will never fade
From the fields of Runnymede.

Millennium Blocker
à Guillaume Le Conquête

Orange
William of Orange
Le homme du Millennium,
The man who won the Battle of Hastings in 1066,
Gave English a running start
By opening the doors to unlimited morphology
Introducing frog talk to the Islanders
From where he'd picked it up in Normandie.
Vandalize!

The powers that piss on
The empty heads of the American public
Tried to convince them that Gutenberg
Was the man of the millennium
Who moved type from China to publish *The Bible.*

They would have been better off fingering Martin Luther.
You have to have something to say before
The means to print it make any difference.

And a language to put it in:
Vern Nacular.

The Tin Island Speculation

From Pliny the Elder to Pliny the Younger
For all the other little Plinys to be

I've been reading a lot of Strabo lately.
I predict the fishermen clad in hides
On the dampened plains of what they call Kent
Will one day put their tongues to steel
And develop a language the world will speak.

I'd get laughed out of the Forum for saying this
In public where the truth is born to be scorned.

Once that happens and it could take
A few thousand years or so
In some other back water of the New English speaking Empire
Some other rude buggers put upon for their insolence
Will start some variation on the irresistible truth
The rest of us won't be able to understand
And make off with the structure of their arrangements.

Independence is fatal but so is life and
Even in captivity syntax rules.

Verbal Dex

(Terity)
Trosity
Adrine

Compare *Han Yu dong ci* with English verbs and those in *Nihongo*.

Peeling off another layer
From the verbal decks I find
The pivotal Mandarin verb
Appoints a time word at the head of the sentence
To locate the action temporally.

The English verb contains the time,
Can indeed locate an action in 128 times and plausibility zones
By adding morphological and phenomenological elements.
The infix of the after byte.
The Agenbyte of Inwit.
The Asshole from El Paso.

Nihongo verbs, coming at the terminus of the expression,
Can change at the last minute the intended message.
The pivot is at the end,
Causing verbal whiplash
And maximizing flexibility.

This could be why Japanese complain so hard when asked
To adhere to the terms of the contract, one composed in English
Where the rules are fixed, when circumstances change.

To the Japanese, changed circumstances change the contract.
In English, you are expected to take the risks of the potential for
Changing circumstances and live with them.

This is the static cling forced onto
Dynamic circumstances.

What to do about speculation without risk?
The preferred method in English of speculating.
Since molecular let alone economic circumstances are constantly
          changing
Where did the insistence on contracts come from?
People who could with superior intelligence and information
Foresee or predict the change in circumstances
And write contracts to reflect the change.
Making themselves the beneficiaries of changing circumstances
Outside the victim's scope.

Dealing with fluctuations in the time value of money.
The Japanese have made money worthless [.5% or .25%].
That has no time value.
It means there is nothing you can do with the money that will make it
Worth more in six months than it is the day you get it.
Deflation.

No wonder the New York and London bankers wring their hands and
Rail at the Japanese to fix their problem.

The Chinese are so adhoc.
Just change the date.
The timing is not right.

The Japanese are hampered by scale, otherwise their system would be
          in charge.
It is the most flexible and the most ruthless
Namely because *Keigo* makes the consequences for the underlings
Too God Damned Bad.

Since *Magna Carta*, the middle class,
Their own kind of underlings
Have usurped the commercial power with the
          Transnational Corporation.
They don't want those consequences.
They want to hold on to what they've got:

Anything piled up at the end of the sentence, dock,
As object of their usufructing verbs.

Time, since it is everywhere, is on the side of
        the Middle Kingdom.
English no longer has a kingdom.

"There is no society," Prime Minister Maggie Thatcher said.
How right she was.
Hao Kan.

Mandarin verbs are pivots, can be adjectives.
Hao Kan, good looking, includes is, no verb, looks good.
I give you my verb
And you may reply upon it.

Try Angular Eyes Ashun
Triangularization

I refamiliarize myself
With the concrete sequentiality (sequential structure)
Of well-made Mandarin sentences.

When the Japanese attempt diplomacy
It's interpreted as patronizing condescension
Because *Keigo*, the Japanese honorific language,
Only operates down and makes
Everything inferior to the speaker,
(If the speaker is in a position to be diplomatic that is.
Speakers coming from the bottom up simply sound obsequious
Because they are pro forma indicted as inferior
The moment they open their mouths.)

The Chinese, with millennia of hard practice,
Look down their own toney noses
At Japanese attempts to emulate their virtues and culture.

From here (in the Pacific Northwest)
Across the North (Wide) Pacific
I see storms approaching
One after the other
An endless profusion and succession of weather
Propelling jackasses in kayaks
Onto the ever nearer western shore.

The Pacific Ocean gets 2 inches narrower every year.
The jet stream operates an endless churn
Of the hydrologic cycle.

I'm beginning to really like my (Iron)
North Pacific Ocean Triangle.

The Open Range
The Closed Sea

The Middle Kingdom

Tied in their mutually exclusive and interdependent knots
The cultures compete
For market share, adherents and industrial capacity.

It's at their capitols where their beliefs
Are strung up on architectural frames
Where the buzz of both
The power of their expression and
Its essential limitations are made utterly clear.

The Imperial Palace in Tokyo
Enfant's DC mall in Washington flanked by
The largest aggluteration of fascist architecture
West of *Le Champs Elysees* and *Der Friedrich Strasse*
Where it crosses at right angles the *Unter den Linden*
Leading to the brick shithouse of *Friedrichstadt*,
While *Tiananmen*
The door to heavenly peace is flanked
By the Forbidden City on the north
And the Great Hall of the People on the west
In the muddled middle of the Middle Kingdom.

I think I was last at the Imperial Palace
Hiking over the drawbridge on the basalted moats
On my way back from interviewing Dr. Doi
The roar of Tokyo all around us,
The small part where the peons are permitted to roam
Unmolested by the royalty and their
Flies in amber motility.

2.
I think I can use the triangular eyes
In a non-Hegelian apocalyptic
Transfer and surge of crude energy.

Nothing is quite as deep as cultural chagrin,
Founded as they all are on the central story of identification as
The chosen people.
If we're so well chosen
How so be it that we are surrounded by the non-chosen?
Who's plan was this to be
Hemmed in on all sides by inferiorities?

The Middle Kingdom expands and contracts.
Its pulsations are equal to its degrees of disorganization
Plus the resistance by the inferiors on the perimeter.
With no intervening power structure or
Distribution of authority (Pye),
The bigger the pulse
The longer the span of power has to reach
From the emperor to the households on the edge.

The MK is in an expansion phase
Will soon control the movement of the
Western Pacific Basin economy through the
Polluted seas of *Dagat.*

England weary of the Europe from which they spawned
Went south and west and around the rest of the world
Taking slaves, setting up tea shops, spawning in turn
The United States of America
An Island with the inclusion of the Canal Panama,
Now the world's largest banana republic,
A bigger British Empire with a bigger cloak of false democracy,
To conceal its expropriating intentions.
The Open Range a Texas southern idea
Brought on horseback from the South to barbed wire
And the naval need to keep the oceans an open range themselves.

Since Tokugawa *Jidai* the waters around Japan have been divided
Into sectors, spheres, delegated out to *Daimyos*
And in the case of Fukuoka to the collective.
This sea is closed; fish elsewhere.

Japanese whalers and shrimpers and every manner
Of other kind of boat in all the waters of the world,
Since the waters near Japan were closed,
The rest of the sea must remain open.
Otherwise how will the energy supply we depend on get here?

Three non-equidistant sets of islands come back to the sea
To see their problems sorted into relationships
With people they barely understand and tolerate
For their own extensive purposes.
Diplomacy is war by other means.
War is diplomacy by other means
Means and ends are war and diplomacy.

(I must quickly look up *The Revelations of the Chill at Appomattox*)

At the moment and for the past 100 years the seas
Have been kept open by Theodore Roosevelt's American Navy
And Admiral Mahan's correct belief that it was the British Navy
That sealed Wellington's victory over Napoleon at Waterloo.
And gave the British Empire the rest of the 19th century.

Two hundred years of unadulterated British and American horseshit
Force fed to the undergunned hither and yon
Like the human targets in the Sudan for the Gatling guns,
The Sioux, the Zulu, the Nazis.

After the battle of Sekigahara, Tokugawa excused the Japanese
From this melee for fourteen generations of medieval family misrule
Until the *Meiji Ishin* and the American Navy under Perry
Brought them back to the table.

Toyotomi Hideoyoshi twice in the decade prior to Sekigahara
Tried to conquer Beijing by invading through Korea,
An elementary organizing of the destructive projections
And focusing them on an exterior enemy once all the
Local enemies had been brought into the fold.

Le Meme Chose took place again after the *Meiji Ishin* industrialization
And the Japanese flirted with conquering China to their dismay,
Nanjing, Harbin, Shanghai, Hiroshima and Nagasaki.

This concrete sequential Japaneselizing of the verb to empire
Didn't work too well, as if the English had thought to commence their
        empire
By first invading Normandie.

The Middle Kingdom was the doormat for a hundred of the past
Two hundred years, the colony of every country we every signed
A treaty with, according to Sun Yatsen.

Mao Zedong activated a premise and made it stick:
To rid China of foreign domination.

Now all China has to do is gradually grow itself out around
The US-Japan 78% control of the Pacific Basin Economy
Until it can control the supply of energy through *Dagat* to *Nihon*
Whence it can advise the imperial puppets in Tokyo
Of the considerable width of the Pacific Ocean and its distance from
Its protection in the form of the American Navy and Air Force,
Since air is only a form of water and planes an ineffective
Form of a ship. A bicycle with wings that can't carry much
Except ballistics which won't win again.

Japan becomes the neutral state,
The Switzerland of the Pacific in *Macassas'* phrase.*
The US doesn't have a base anymore and Asia belongs to China.

At this point the Rubes from the South who admire their navy
And misread their own history at every fine point
Will probably go ballistic and attempt to
Win this war the old fashioned way.

They will lose.
The laws of thermodynamics apply to everybody.

The African, Mexican, American grip on their own continent
Will be reinforced on their knees defending the western edge
From invasion.

zhe shi buke beimian de. [xiangfan de]

3.
War is the attempt to control the economic future by force.
There are a gazillion ways to apply force that haven't been dreamed of
      yet.
The old wars are over.
In the empire of the US they are fought over and over again.
You can actually rent uniforms for Confederate Battles and play
      particular parts.
Nothing sells like glory.

It is the new wars that have to be won.
Who's eating my lunch.
What will my lunch consist of and who will prepare it.
How long can I rely on these arrangements.
What is reinforcing them.
Who's after my lunch?

*The way the Japanese persist in mispronouncing MacArthur's name.
Anyone for Cutty Sark?

When People Walked Out of Natural History Talking

Language and behavior are two phases of the same phenomena. Language separated people from natural history. Cultural history is the story of people using language. Society is a linguistic echo. If we can talk about it it is likely already over. Language generation to produce a future we can live with more comfortably is a mild obsession rooted in perpetual discontent. Circumstances change constantly. So too should people. But change how, to what style, to what degree, in which direction.

If thought were possible, thinking would be illegal. Producing futures is something the Indo-European languages excel at with their if/would structure. The more alternatives that can be generated, the more choices, the closer the model gets to being one that can be activated.

The alphabet storage and retrieval system facilitates this process. Ideographic writing systems create impediments to abstraction and reinforce the daily connections.

The Trans-Siberian railroad is an example of if/is rather than if/would.

You get the kind of world you think it is. Change your mind. Change the world.

The Question of Lines

What if a horizontal line above is heavier than one below?

Will it not crush it, won't they all sag to the point that only the heavy lines are visible?

I prefer vertical lines, stripped like banners from the upper right to the trailers at the bottom of the page, like good Japanese. It makes the *hiragana* useful. Each line hangs like a fish in the market, has to hang from a solid beginning, won't crush anything below it because it is all it.

These tragedies are not organized.

Get a back hoe and crowbar a few Koreans in.

New Directions: I leave to the scavengers the open question of whether or not their poetry was worth reprinting in the second place, be it old or new.

The purpose of Appaloosas is disposition.

They knew they were ornaments the moment they were foaled.

Ping Ping had dreams he kept under wraps.

What a strange thing it is to be a body, all 206 bones of it.

But hey, it's all working. It's the angle of attack that is missing. If polarized over the North Pacific, how to stay grounded. Or is that just another way to keep from taking sides? The thing with literacy is if you take sides with known losers you violate the **laws of association**. The firing squad mentality. Staying off of all sides appeals to the historian in me. My inner historian at that. The appeal of the drama is greater than the history of the future combined. What's so ridiculous in all this long distance trading of goods and services is that it violates the **laws of peasantry**: get it close to home and trade for equal value. The real law to obey is **the law sound makes**.

The Structure of History

How structure operates, how it works and why it matters.

Structure predicts output. Nothing sustainable will happen that is not supported by structure. Structure is the elaboration of belief expressed in language. I used the phrase "how structure operates," which could also be an independent clause, because history is a branch of epistemology.

The Open Range:

The Empire of the United States is a constitutional plutocracy. It developed a system of laws based on a constitution designed to distribute political power in such a way that it would always be controlled by a determined minority of moneyed interests. Its democratic front is a masquerade for public relations purposes.

At the end of World War Two when the Empire became a world power, enlarging its base from being more than an American power and a Pacific power, it adopted a twin economic engine. Not understanding the weaknesses of its business cycle and having blundered its way through a twelve year economic depression, the proffered cure was to stimulate domestic demand, now called consumerism, a political construct in its own right, and to search for and develop foreign markets for goods manufactured in the United States.

This bifold revolution stood on its head the nineteenth century domestic economic standard of frugalism while at the same time forced the United States into a global diplomatic role from its previous and sincere flirtation with isolationism. This policy adopted during the Truman Administration has not been altered since.

Civics teachers pound the lie into the heads of American school children, whom they hope someday to draft or otherwise coerce into the military to protect this scheme of things, that the Constitution is the basis for American success.

The religious success of the Empire, which I heard expressed yesterday on TV by a no doubt sincere veteran of the colonial war against Viet Nam, that the healing wall, a traveling replica of the Viet Nam War Memorial in Washington D.C., reminded him that he had to make a pilgrimage to Washington to see the real thing, that it was his Mecca, makes a complete fusion of a military symbol into a religious icon.

In recent history, the last two thousand years, the religious construct that the Empire of the United States most resembles is the one flung across North Africa, the Middle East clear into Indonesia, and into Europe by the descendants of Mohammed. It is also related to the spread of Roman military culture throughout the Mediterranean Basin and the previous thrust of Alexander with the Hellenic civilization to the East.

The success of the Empire of the United States can be attributed largely to the initial low overhead. They absconded with the lion's share of a continent rich with natural resources from its hapless Neolithic defenders. Genocide is the first cause of American success. Its relative isolation, being several thousand nautical miles from enemies of sufficient scale to do it serious harm, is the second most significant structural component.

The Empire of the United States is, in time present, only the elaboration of the English mercantile system that bankrolled the British Empire. From its piratical beginnings in the sixteenth century with the capstone of the defeat of the Spanish Armada in 1588, the British Empire put the finishing touches on its chief rival, Napoleonic France, with Wellington's victory at Waterloo.

For the rest of the nineteenth century, British control of the oceans with its navy, directed traffic toward London. By the end of the Victorian period, the unintended consequences of this economic exchange with the rest of the world had redistributed the means of manufacture elsewhere and England declined for fifty years, skillfully maneuvering itself to a position where the United States, its most successful eighteenth century progeny, could make a basket catch of its policies and intentions. With the Atlantic Charter agreed to in secret by Roosevelt and Churchill, the power of the Empire and its literal military bases was clandestinely transferred.

Time present, the southern policy makers of the Empire of the United States, for the British sympathies throughout the nineteenth century were largely with the South, including support for the Confederacy during the American Civil War, act as if the Empire of the United States was an empire on which the sun will never set.

Naiveté is only one of this flawed opinion's problems. The unstable and symbiotic relationship between the American military apparatus and the transnational corporations is based on the bifold revolution adopted in the late 1940s: stimulate domestic consumption and expand foreign markets. Without foreign markets to protect for the benefit of the shareholders of transnational corporate stock, the American military could successfully defend North America with a tenth of its current appropriations.

The structural flaw of transnational corporate capital is its reliance on the profit motive which demands absolute growth to shield itself from inefficiency and the essential entropic destruction of resources, such as clean air, fresh water, viable soil. The Roman Empire collapsed when the hinterland lost interest in Rome's preoccupations.

Believing, however mistakenly, that they can take for granted the transatlantic economic transfers between North America and a rapidly uniting Europe, the Empire is focused on its relatively shaky investments in the Pacific Basin Economy.

Because of their aggressive, antientropic blindness, the Empire of the United States has obliged itself to carry on the by now two hundred year old war the British started with China for control of the Pacific Basin Economy.

North American has sound superior geographical structural positioning to win defensive wars, almost literally forever, if the policies agreed to by its leadership do not squander, as they have been, both of its most valuable resources: those found in the natural world and the goodwill of the people.

The incredibly expensive and counterproductive colonial wars in Korea and Viet Nam used up a great deal of the residual goodwill of the American people, to say nothing of the indefensible potlatch of the energy, air, soil and water. Southern diplomats, an oxymoron smeared with ginger, will try to keep the war focused on the profit stream for American and London based banks and corporations.

The weakness of the American transpacific grip has been demonstrated in Korea, Viet Nam, the abdication and attempt to make the Philippines a neo-colonial from a literal colonial construct, etc. Their major military and economic base remains the Japanese islands subdued at the end of World War Two.

The Closed Sea

The Japanese structural problem is obvious. Their economic engine and its constituent role in the American Japanese transnational economy, where 78% of the APEC transfers are between American and Japanese interests, circa 1996, is 80% dependent on imported sources of energy. Due to ancient and dithering animosities between Russian and Japan, revived in part and kept alive by memories of the Russo-Japanese war of 1904, Siberian energy has not been available to Japan. Most of Japan's imported energy passes on tankers through the South China Sea.

The Middle Kingdom

In twenty to thirty years when the Chinese economy begins to seriously rival the one dominated presently by the United States, Chinese pressure on the Japanese energy supply, will alter policy in Tokyo, first in the direction of neutrality, finally in the direction of tilt of Tokyo from New York to Beijing. The Japanese will do this reluctantly. They would prefer an arms length relationship with the United States to the cheek by jowl relationship with China. But the Japanese, structurally, are professional victims. The Japanese honorific language, the *Keigo* in *Nihongo*, is a razor strop to hone victimship.

Chinese structural superiority is based on their development of interior lines. They can win this war simply by adding to them and developing a navy one fourth the size of that necessary to the success of the United States. Mandarin, a phonetically impoverished language of concrete sequentiality, is the perfect vehicle for the alternately expanding and contracting pulsations that have characterized Chinese history for several thousand years. It reinforces operations on interior lines.
Change belief, change behavior, change languages.

Objections and Where to Stack Them

Composing a work like *Across the North Pacific* leaves me absolutely giddy with freedom since it will be practically completely misunderstood initially I am free to do exactly as I please. I am a soul mate with Nietzsche here, writing for the future trees who have less of an invested interest in misunderstanding everything for commercial and religious purposes. And Ford Madox Ford who once said he was leaving London because nobody there understood what he said. I render and reveal. I am not in London, one time capitol of the English speaking world, nor even in New York, current capitol of the third world capitalists and centre of publishing in the English speaking world. I could lean also on the withered stalk of one of Baudelaire's *Fleurs du Mal* and realize that those who'll understand me will divine me and it would be fruitless to heap up explanations for those who cannot.

Composing this in English, language of my native tongue—I was not born speaking English but the people I was born to were speaking it when I got there—I cannot think of a single serious publisher broadminded enough to overcome their own confusion and ignorance long enough to give this work a chance. New Directions never did anything this new and nothing new of any kind since about 1960. Their work was half Modernism and half Postmodernism, both now museum pieces and the ghastly feasting sites of selected graduate students.

I cannot neglect the asset less youngsters in the harness with me trying to pull some sense out of the taffy in this mixing bowl. Nor will I dwell on the delicious irony of the most public of pertinent ideas being forced into secrecy by the reactionary recidivism of current popular culture.

The upper classes in English, doing so superficially well these days having mastered speculation without risk, want their children to have the best education almost universally for the purposes of mastering obfuscation of their genuine circumstances. They are on what they'd like to continue believing is the perpetual parabola bow curve of Manifest Destiny. Anything that doesn't support their self-aggrandized superiority is misinterpreted as naysaying propaganda. They have so poisoned the shallow well of ideas in English that they will be brought to heel ignorant of their own excesses.

Enough about the idiot detractors in English. Nobody in Chinese will have the tools to mount an objection until the work gets translated. Their primary problem is how to run an effective and inexpensive bluff. That's what will keep time on their side. So too the Japanese objection. They want in their heart of hearts for there to be a continued Enlightenment where faux democracy as practiced by the *Juminto* can thrive under the old time nuclear umbrella of plantation crackpots. They have less in common with the Chinese than Americans do, superficialities of their conservative and cobbled together writing system aside. Expect them to resist understanding, let alone appreciating for what it is, their supporting role. They are youngsters who want to be a star only to mature into the realization that the firmament is filled already. Their language insists on their superiority while their lack of mass has rendered them a compliment.

Li Ping Deer's Address to the Halfbreeds
From the Province of Sardonia

It's time for me to tune this up.
No point in trying to explain myself.

Blow the cover of the Chinese.
Insult the superiority of the Japanese.

What it will do for the speakers of English
Will be every person for itself.

Pump up the Spanish
Alamogordo
Fat cottonwood in a wet spring.

The North Star

This is not Polaris
But a oneman satellite
In permanent geosynchronous orbit
Over the North Pacific
Trying simultaneously to see and understand
All three great North Pacific cultures at the same time.

The Open Range

Opportunities in Disintegration

All my life I've wanted to write great poetry.
The great poetry in English is all about
Disintegration.
King Lear, Wordsworth's *Immortality Ode,* Yeats,
Suggesting survival of the opportunist.
Opportunities in disintegration
Is my theme.

In the middle of disintegrating structure
Held together piecemeal by clueless conservatives
There are a few things worth keeping intact.
The love of family and friends is paramount.
Love of state is an unsustainable projection,
Propped up with religious fervor
To protect the dominant minority and ruling class
From the consequences of their excess.

How far can cooperation in English be extended
Before it meets the financed arms of the state?

Yet I can't close a poem with an open-ended question.
Yeats did.

Too bad the rough beast on its merry way to Bethlehem
Overshot the runway.
The flight from oppression
Leads through towns whose names
Will one day resonate with love.

We will not surrender language
To attorneys and the legislature.
The function of the legislature is to concoct policy
That won't upset Christians with the truth.
English in the hands of statists
Is a holding action for the ugly side of love.

It bumped up against the water
Of the North Pacific Ocean,
Straddling it with glee until
The unintended consequences of commerce
Swamped its little boat.

English Think

To write about the ongoing war between
The speakers of English and the speakers of Mandarin
For control of the Pacific Basin Economy,
I express myself for the moment in English,
Trying to keep my point of view
Geosynchronously positioned over the approximate midpoint
Of the North Pacific Ocean.

The Battle of Midway between
The Japanese forces of Hirohito and the American Roosevelt Navy
During the Pacific War against the upstart Japanese
Was in the line of vision and of fire.

Hawaii, on which volcanic sand
I've never set foot,
Was amalgamated into the British Plantation system
By Republicans from the United States
Once Grover Cleveland was out of office and
As soon as William Jennings Bryan was hung
Out to dry on a cross of gold
Bearing his free silver cross of freedom
Crucified on a metallic double cross.

Ordinary people have little to do with it.
They fill the body bags.
They slide off the decks of sinking ships.
They pick the pineapple and sew the Nike soles on shoes.
It is a war of systems
Manipulated by aristocrats.

2
If ordinary people were making policy in North America
The war would be seen for what it is:
A design to increase the net worth of the
Shareholders of the transnational corporations
Headquartered in New York, London and colonial Tokyo.
It produces jobs as an unfortunate byproduct of the profit process.

The first English oar dipped in water,
Bred into their hands by their Viking past,
Wound up off Kowloon and Hong Kong
Peddling Indian Opium to ordinary Chinese
For an immense and traditionally drugged product and profit.

Billions race daily around electronic circuit boards
Tracking the lost profit, speculating for an opening.

It is memorial day weekend and the dead American soldiers
Lay down with something "older than man,
Wet shale gives off the smell of,
Is it a love of, petroleum?" Edward Smith asked,
An American soldier-poet of intelligent reluctance,
Speaking Vietnamese thirty-five years ago
In a still officially unacknowledged American colonial fiasco.

3
There are children, my own and yours, who suffer and will suffer
The inescapable consequences of the hidden war.
Without the outrageous profits made possible by depriving
The working class of its value-added,
Trans-Pacific commerce would not be profitable at all,
Once the energy required to move the goods is factored in to
The expense of protecting the privileges of the privileged class
And their bullshit rendition of free trade
Supported at all points by a camouflaged disregard
For the irreversible depletion of natural resources and
The destruction of the natural world.
The conservatives could not bear any
Full social cost accounting.

The dropping of the shroud of the Universal State on the
Weak ideals of the American system
Produced an empire hybrid of unprecedented corruption.
The traditional mechanisms for resistance have been neutered

Out of the system at the insistence of the plutocracy.
The state is prepared to shoot to kill
Anybody even dreaming of getting out of
The neo-Confederate Universal State including
Randy Weaver's wife, son, and dog,
The Branch Davidians,
The Freemen of Montana,
The Symbionese Liberation Army,
The Republic of Texas.

The bottom line thought in English think is
Expressed in the principle the conservatives follow to spiral us off
The face of the flat earth:

If there is a position to the right of the one under discussion
I want to go there.

The (K) Celtic Triad

In the forests and on the beaches of Northwestern Europe
Before God and Caesar in any order got to them
The Celtic Triad had a king in the middle
Flanked by jester in charge of jokes
And a poet to make sure that the truth
Didn't escape unnoticed.

Beware of role confusion.

Kings are in charge of the messy business of
Life and death.
Jesters charge the immune system with the unholy
Humor of it all.
Poets will make you weep
Just when you need to be most strong.

The real danger is from jokers who think they're poets.

1968

There were two watershed years in the twentieth century:
1929 when speculators leaped from tall buildings
To meet the concrete consequence of their fantasies as
The roaring of the twenties simmered down into the Great Depression
      whine;
1968 when the country and the empire clashed for good.

I have a photograph from the 1940s when I was born
Of my brother Don, our dog Skip and I
Taken after World War Two but before 1950
In Grandma Gray's front yard.

I am tousled and determined in such pre-school love
And this determination has stuck with me
Even though an entire generation of idealists
Had the idealism mashed out of us by 1968.

I walk out onto the front porch in the middle of the night
To listen to the La Niña rain and the wind through the trees.
Many years ago I heaped river stones beneath the rain gutter
So during storms a man made waterfall would splash off the rocks
To remind me of the sound nature used to make
Before climate got absorbed as just another cost of doing business.

1968 dawned upon me in Puerto Vallarta, Jalisco,
And took leave of me in Salt Lake City, actually Murray, Utah.
Meanwhile between the parenthesis I went bananas in Berkeley,
A city I'd been trying for four years to get to,
The most intellectual and politically progressive enclave
In an empire totally nuttied up by the War on Viet Nam
As the long shadow cast by Ike and the ignorant CIA in Saigon's
Picking up of the pieces the French were only too glad to drop in
Dien Bin Pheu, smothered the natural light of America.

The people fought the government for three days at the
Oakland Army Base, trying to stop troop trains.

Never had it been so impossible to make sense in public
In a public bereft of newspapers, free speech,
Adults in positions of authority who hadn't kowtowed
To an empire's madness with the middle name of lie.

Why shouldn't a depressed population take up its individual problems
With a bewildering array of counter productive drugs?
Alcohol, Tobacco, Heroin, Marijuana, Money, TV, Rock, Cocaine,
Because their is no door way out that could be successfully
Knocked down with anger.

My brother, our dog and I
Look as if we were having a good time.
The dog is always happy.
My brother was damned glad to have gotten back from
World War Two in the Pacific alive.
Me, I didn't know any better in 1947.
More like the dog than anybody else
Going to get used to being kicked around
Determined from the outset to survive and be happy.

If the door can't be knocked down with anger
Pried open with ideas
Or disappeared with love
The other fatal trap of transcendentalist psychosis
Appears like a conversation cloud in a cartoon
To suck the unwary up.

All the major religions I know of have a scuttle to the attic
Through which top up rather than top down trap door
The superior types escape to lord it over the rest of us.
The view from this mystical heaven ain't interesting,
Whether Sufi, Zen, or Trappist Monk.

Left here, facing drugs, political irrelevance, religious manipulation,
Tempted with romantic slash and burn approaches

What to do when all apparent choices lead nowhere?
Body out with feelings and straight talk song
In as many tones as a warbler can get to.

Discover how things are.
Don't be misled by religious fantasy
Economic exploitation
Government manipulation
Druggy fuzzing of the edges
Parental disapproval
Lack of funding or
Failure of nerve.

Make friends
Cement alliances
Listen to your body
Hear the music
Sing the songs
O wild one, you are it.

The Northwest Passage

The level of the ocean rises and falls
Under the gravitational pull of the romantic moon and
Other even farther out stoned and gaseous bodies.

When the United States became a Pacific power and
Transoceanic empire by annexing Hawaii
Bludgeoning Aguinaldo and the Philippines
Absconding with Panama from Columbia
Before William Howard Taft
Rammed through the Panama Canal
At Teddy Roosevelt's blustered urging
North America was still a continent.
Cut in to a peninsula in the 20th century
When ice breakers prowl the seal infested seas
Between Baffin Island and the Bering Strait
With typical overbearing technical aplomb
Giving those riders on the open range
Another useless techno fix way out.
(There is yet to be a Northwest Passage worthy of the name)

North America's a Turtle Island moving slowly with only two sides.
The Atlantic Ocean is a yard wide with a European capitol in olde
        New York,
Once New Amsterdam, now mayored by an Italian cop
With isolated contingents cheek to cheek of
Jews, Irish, Puerto Ricans, Italians, Chinese, Africans, and
A duke's mixture of poor white trash taking up the slack and
Filling in the blanks by melting their pots and smoking it
        chicken and all.

Out on the West Coast or back on the West Coast or
Up and down the West Coast I've traveled from
Horseshoe Bay in Beautiful British Columbia
To the wide Rio Lempa in colonial El Salvador,
Watching the curvature of the ocean cover the earth in between
With wavy water from Wreck Beach, Cape Flattery, Shi Shi Beach,
Ruby Beach, Ocean Shores, Long Beach, Astoria, Seaside,

Cape Meares, Cape Lookout, Cape Kiwanda, Depoe Bay,
The Oregon Dunes, Cape Perpetua, Crescent City, Mendocino,
Sonoma, Point Reyes, Stilson Beach, Big Bad Bolinas,
The Emeryville Mudflat across the polluted San Francisco Bay,
Point Lobos, Pacific Palisades, Monterey, Big Sur,
Moros Bay, Pebble Beach, Santa Barbara, Venice, Carlsbad
San Diego, Ensenada, Guaymas, Mazatlan, San Blas, Puerto Vallarta,
Conchas Chinas, Mismaloya, Yelapa, Bahia de Bandereas, Zihuatanejo,
Acapulco, Puerto Escondido, Tapachula, to Acajutla and beyond.

Could you get the impression I was trying to get off
This island if only for a few feet into the water in every direction.
From the other side it still looks *tai hen* strange
From *Ibaraki Ken* or out the window coasting into *Narita*,
Kamakura, Katsurahama on *Shikoku, Setoniakai, Shimonoseki,*
Beppu, Miyazaki, Kagoshima, Pusan and the Islands around Hong Kong
And Kowloon where China meets the world on regurgitated terms.

This be two arcs of the northern semi-circle of the ring of fire,
Drawn together by their compound interest in the Hawaiian Islands
And other atolls, coral reefs and volcanic upthrusts as will support
An air base, a harbor, an army barracks, an American Indian Ira Hayes
Helping his Marine Corps Comrades raise Old Glory on Iwo Jima
          under fire.

The American claim to the Pacific Ocean economy
Will be under fire as long as they assert it.
The ukulele boogie of Waikiki
Was drowned out by Kamikaze pilots singing *Tora! Tora! Tora!*
On their way to a molten lava meltdown
On a pineapple plantation,
Tiger! Tiger! Tiger! burning bright on the bottom of Pearl Harbor Bay.

Nihon metastasized into an ally of obsequious reluctance
In the fire bombing of Fukuoka and Tokyo
While Hiroshima and the Christian Catholics of Nagasaki
Mushroomed into oblivion by atomic bombs.

Weary of trying to make Japan over
Into a socialist democracy,

The Korean War induced MacArthur,
The would be Julius Caesar of the Pacific
And his CIA Trumanoid replacements,
To promote the conservative coalition, *Juminto*,
Which with truly minor exceptions has governed
This Switzerland of the Pacific ever since.

The Japanese had millions of reasons to be astonished
By the lenient terms of their occupation
And look askance at their chances when the Chinese
Reassert *Zhonguoan* Hegemony over them
By proximity and powerful straddle of
The boatloads of energy on their way to Nagoya
Thru the Straits of Malacca and *Dagat*, the South China Sea.

If the Americans weren't speaking English which got them this far
And into which the questions that might save their superior position
Simply can't be put,
They'd be on their way to saving themselves
By rebuilding a railroad system of magnetic levitation
Full scale development of zero resistant materials
Let alone cold Mormon fusion
To rein in their profligate wastage of energy
Before the laws of thermodynamics put them in a jail of their own
        creation.

The Northwest is a passage to a point of view
Which takes no position while maintaining its intention
Of telling the truth which remains in neutral and
Can be used like a scientific principle
By any side recognizing its practical application.

When the conniving politicians and their overfed generals,
Not to mention their corrupt capitalist income stream,
Have been brought to heel like fascists before them
To judgments more complete and equally deserving
As those pounded out at Nuremberg,
The air in a few awake minds will clear
A river of light to carry the truth literally thru all things.

Pahsimeroi Eki

Pahsimeroi Eki begins to take shape
In imaginary union spliced between
Shoshoni and Nihongo.
Formerly there was no Eki in Pahsimeroi.
This is the way to the Pahsimeroi station.

The Eki Kanji has its parts
Contributing to the union.
It is a horse up against a flute,
A shaku hatchi in fact,
A call for transportation.

A left handed horse with binocular vision
A right handed flute with erotic overtones
Playing its tune in the great outdoors
Beyond the Granger's Hall in May
In a Uto-Aztecan desert.

While only the station is stationary,
Everything else takes on the character of constant change.
The station is molecular morphemes traveling
In stationary formation
Composing Pahsimeroi Eki.

Pahsimeroi's a river by definition
With a single grove of trees.
Pahsimeroi's a valley of the union
Between horses and music.
Pahsimeroi Eki's where we hear
How the West was lost
In the gasp where the world begins.

My father used to whistle for his horses.
The bright ones came galloping at the sound.
He had no flute but horseback transportation,
To escape from English into sound.

I need to get out of here.
Can you call me a horse.

You're a horse, Pahsimeroi Eki.
We've been stalled at the station
For a long time.

The Prelude to Transportation

Pahsimeroi Eki seems to be "The Prelude to Transportation."
His will be a character in constant motion,
A Heraclitan DNA neuralinguistic gene splicer
Executing an escape from English.

Dionysus digs the Rubicon.

The Echo Nobody Hears

Originality goes unrecognized
Often enough that it stays pertinent
To keep on pointing it out.

If you say something beautiful
And no one believes it
Would you be better off
To keep your mouth shut?

Hardly a moment goes by
When an original voice
Isn't being smothered out by
The ordinary, the predictable, the safe.

At Pahsimeroi Eki with the sound bouncing back
From the tallest peaks of the Lost River Range
Only the sonar of a bat out of hell
Could keep you from flying into the debris.

By the process of echolocation
The high speed flyers
Recognize the proximity of solid things
And gracefully avoid them.

A horse, a horse
My kingdom for a horse
Is a bargain King Richard
Would have accepted too late and yet

Surrounded as we all have been
By the disintegrating structure of our own power plays
There comes the moment every protagonist dreads
When he or she would trade it all in
Just for a way out.

Reprimanding the Species

Downtown at Pahsimeroi Eki
My hometown without a town,
We're only one valley left of where
Lewis & Quark
First set white feet
Into the Pacific drainage in
The Lemhi Valley of *The Book of Mormon.*

Every little river
Has a tributary full of
Topsoil and salmon
To share with the sea.

The sea at hand is the North Pacific.
We get back from there through the Columbia Gorge
Over unbreachable Snake River dams
Up the River of No Return
Into the Pahsimeroi tributary to
All of the above in broken flow
Cumulating in 303 sized tins of canned salmon.

As long as there's plenty of which on the shelf
How can salmon be endangered
Declaims Idaho's dingbat congresstwat
The disHonorable Helen Chenowith,
A brazen adulterer not that long ago
Along with a few hundred other rag doll Republicans
But still impeachers of blowjob Bill.

Going down the river would be too good
For the wasted political us.

"The Solid Man Muldoon"

Once you've seen some
Of the rest of the world
The mountains of Idaho
Look better and better.

They look better now
Than they ever did when
Lonely teenagers arrived back home
Saddle sore way after dark.

Muldoon Canyon lies between
Lake Creek and Star Hope canyons
Draining the northwest side of
Smiley Mountain into Copper Basin.

Across Copper Basin nodding out
In the saddle as my father led
Tony and the other horses
In the middle of the night,

I was five years old
Holding on to the horn
While Coyotes called to one another
From horizon to horizon canopied with stars.

This is where
Big Lost River begins
From lost water falling
Out of the snow flaked sky.

Twenty-three years later
I was back in the saddle
Riding 50 miles one day
From Chamberlin Basin to Taylor Ranch.

Only saw one
Other man all day,
Starting in the dark
And arriving in the dark,

Leading six head of horses
Through choke cherry groves
On trails piled up
With wet bear scat.

Muldoon is a metaphor
For self reliance
In a co-dependent catastrophe
Unraveling in time.

I am not the global
Village explainer.
I parse the echoes of manics
Who could stop talking if they tried.

I only deal
With the North Pacific Quadrant,
At most a quarter
Of our rotundity.

The North Atlantic Quadrant
Is a British triangle
Of slavery drugs and finished goods
Washed down with Barbadian Rum.

The Hurricanes boil out of Africa
South of the doldrums
Filled with the cries of
Africans and horses drowning,

Intent on hosing down
Andrews Air base and Charleston,
Blowing some insurance companies right out of town,
The Homestead, Florida Act indeed.

'Twas McGrath who said in '73
I seemed to him
So much to be
"The Solid Man Muldoon."

Traditional

I was relieved to learn that once
The swearing in of the President had taken place
With his left hand on *The Bible*
As soon as the right hand came down
From where it had been raised to take the
Oath of office
The new President would be handed the leather book
With the nuclear codes:

One hand on *The Bible*
And a finger on the trigger.

Final Pass Over Doublespring

The pass over Doublespring's the fastest
Way to get back to Pahsimeroi
Way back to when my family first set foot
Into the August hills of Idaho.

Going over Doublespring lifts my heart
Above the attack, above timberline
Only 8300 feet and some change
Above the Pacific beaches.

But in these sagebrush hills and rocky mountains
The last place in America to be exploited
The last kid on the block to know
Has finally found out.

In isolated montaigne splendor
Horseback against the thieves of time
Chinese stirrups holding my feet firm
The earth swings into focus.

The Beautiful Blue Pacific

The beautiful blue Pacific makes me wonder
If all those mountains left behind
Really mean all that much

Of the sand and boulders on Ruby Beach
Lead the eye across the water
To the flat back of Destruction
Island.

We were thirty years younger low-riding across
The Olympic Peninsula,
Along the shores of Crescent Lake,
Looking for the rain forest
Where the fronds of ferns unfurl and grow.

One of us was AWOL.
Another left his family for a day.
The driver was going crazy.
It was the first time I'd been out of town
Since moving to Seattle in 1966.

The ocean gives us edge
And our bearings back
To boulders draped with seaweed.
The beautiful blue Pacific
Sucks us home.

North Pacific Ocean Drone

Sea breeze blowing sand in my face
At forty knots an hour.
Is the ocean roaring?
What is the right word to describe the sound,
The word for what the ocean says?

Ed Cameron who reminded me of our meeting
Thirty-six years before and counting
Claims to never pay attention to it, said,
"The ocean is white noise."
The waves are all on the same frequency
Creating
A solid string of sound.

Facing the Sea

In Memory of Charles Olson

No poets are ever going to superimpose
An ideal political system onto the people of North America
Because politics is the art of the possible
Not the possibilities of art.

There is another deeper reason
That our imaginations can't get to while designing
A method for any group larger than ten.

The kernel is contained in your spurning of Toynbee,
The one man who made a saturation job of history,
Not that he had been taking your advice on saturation,
And learned more about it than anyone, even you, would care to hear.

If you had heard him you'd have recognized in his extrapolations of
The universal state
The quagmire tar baby of North America in your time.

Universal state's are negative institutions,
Coming into being after a military knockout blow.
Toynbee didn't invent the phrase for our benefit,
But he uses it accurately to describe the condition of this empire.

Conditions which lead Thomas "Tip" O'Neil,
Onetime Speaker of the House of Representatives
During the Reagan rampage which he supported
—The bipartisan bailout of Social Security on the backs of the
        working poor—
When the House had a 100 vote majority of Democrats,
Southern conservatives who hadn't switched to the Republicans yet,
Just another daffy Irish Catholic from Massachusetts,
To say: "All politics is local,"

Which means desperate, self-serving, adhoc,
Which means in his own picayune way O'Neil'd have understood
Toynbee's description of our political dilemma.

Actually we have a choice and dilemmas are limited to
An Aristotelian fricassee of either or.

Our choices are:
Support the state and act like you enjoy and deserve the benefits it
        confers;
Revolt like romantics and attempt with futility to establish political
        independence;
—The Olsonian choice—or
Work on your spirituality.

Which is why I face the sea this morning
300 miles inland and still swayed by the tides
Of indifference as they wash and lap upon us.

No one on the land who speaks this language
Is making any sense at all about what's happening to us.

The spirit is more appealing than the caucus of compromise.
Even when it promises to build
An organic new system in the carcass of the old,
It's still deficient in appeal when held to the heat of art.

Armed primarily with wits and art
We make our way in the world.

It is this great new clash for control of
The lake of the Pacific that appeals to me.
A mountain boy, once, and
Now
The old man from the mountains
Checking in.

Deciding Years

Year of Decision, homage to DeVoto
1846 when James K. Polk and Zachary Taylor
Took Mexico and the empire
Fixated on the west.

Fifty years later the imperialists
Finally rid of Cleveland the Republicans
Knowing Mexico let alone Oregon would never be enough
Annexed Hawaii to "save it from foreign intervention"
Then took their empire of ironic slaughter
On to Aguinaldo and the Philippines.

1946 a hundred years of empire padding
Globalized itself face to face full circle
With the secret governments of NSC and CIA.

I get fascinated by entire countries going broke
In the pigpen of empire,
It can't be defended and is
Pointless to attack.

The empire has had one president named Truman
For 54 years into 2001 and one policy rarely divagated from:
Increase domestic consumption and search for foreign markets.

Consumer imperialism—
What a waste of the few good ideas
The 18th century American enlightenment codified in
The Bill of Rights
Was, past tense, deservedly famous for.

Free Lance Pheidippides on the
Disinclined Plains of Marathon

The speakers of English are going to lose
The next hundred year war with the Chinese
For control of the Pacific Basin Economy.

The English eclipse will become apparent
When the Chinese economy is large enough
To control the energy supply to Japan.

Without Japan as a military base and industrial theme park
Of the transnational economy incorporated in New York
The Empire of America will no longer be *thee* Asian power.

Who cares?
Our progeny living in an impoverished and
Harassed North America subject to invasion will.

That's when they'll begin to think of me
As a free-lance Pheidippides
On the disinclined Plains of Marathon.

The Disintegrating English Pronoun We

"We hold these truths to be self-evident, that all men [women] are created equal, that they are endowed by their Creator with certain unalienable Rights, that among these are Life, Liberty and the pursuit of happiness [property]." So goes the deservedly famous second sentence of the American Declaration of Independence with the bracketed exceptions: No one in the eighteenth century would have included women among those possessing unalienable rights, or for that matter poor white men and any men other than white. Jefferson cunningly swapped out the word property for the more usefully general happiness. When the American government and the rich white men who run it as a constitutional plutocracy use the word "we" among themselves, everybody knows who and what is being referred to. When they address the mass of Americans outside the loops of power with the pronoun "we," it is clear they are planning some public manipulation. Bipartisan as an adjective usually means something especially criminal is about to take place, since it implies that both factions are expected to benefit from the results at the expense of the people.

Who are we? How did we get to be this way? What if anything can we do about it? How will we know if we're getting anywhere? What difference do we make?

The Americans in pursuit of the rights of Englishmen separated hemselves from England with a muddled victory in the American Revolutionary War. Two hundred and a few odd years and a dozen wars later, the American government fights its wars with hired mercenaries, not volunteers or draftees from the general population. Oddballs like H. Ross Perot of Texas can hire his own army, much as Roman entrepreneurs used to, and send them off on military missions. With several major colonial wars already fought against Asians in Asia, the American government will have to fight its future Asian wars with mercenaries also. There is no "we" here. The benefits of the transnational corporate economy accrue to the shareholders of those corporations, not the public. It is futile to fight a war of aggression such as the colonial ten-year episode in Viet Nam as if the soldiers had a stake in the outcome, no matter how absurd the ideological paint used to vilify the enemies. The great American poet and draft resister Robert Grady Head wrote down the way the conflict would be settled when he wrote: "forge another army that takes its orders from the bottom up." So will we, whoever we are.

Empire Is a State of Mind

Empire is a state of mind
Unconducive to patriotism
Generally reserved for nation states
Cobbled together by Bismarck, Lincoln, Garibaldi,
All upstaged 250 years earlier by Tokugawa,
Now reviving loyalty in the provinces.

The United States of America the country is dead.
It is totally surrounded and no longer the most important part of
The United States of America the Empire

So many men let alone women
Go to bed still thinking of the US of A
As a country yet let alone as
"The greatest poem" according to Walt "the derelict" Whitman.

Their mistaken perception is hard to shake.
Whadda ya want to do about it?
You talkin' to me?
Didja hear the news?

2
Je, the Interrogative

Je hear the news?
Je get the money?
Je pay the piper?
Je Jack the Ripper up his sleeve?

Je is the all purpose contraction
Leading to birth of a new language
Is short for "did you?" answer the questions?

Je have time for this?
Je think you can live without it?
Je feel like getting shaggy?
Je want to hear the rest of the story?

The Ethics of Generalization, Deletion and Distortion
a law firm of linguistic relativity

"We're already beyond everything we have words for." Neitzsche

Ethics brings to a close
Departing sorrow
For unacted on genuine impulses.

The by product of language's three reductions,
Generalization,
Deletion, and
Distortion,
Leaves people struggling to make sense.

If Chomsky-like you try to stay ahead of the trinity
You make up in thoroughness what you lose in timeliness,
You actually fall behind time and
The world goes on without you speechless.

I can take you through it one thread at a time
Until it's as tightly woven as an
Isfahan carpet,
The knots close together and
Cleverly out of sight
On the bottom of the carpet
Facing the floor
Below which the unseen foundation
Makes a platform of structure
And holds up whatever it is
You think you're living in.

The best generalizations are light bulbs at the end of
A judiciously chosen set of facts.

What you choose to delete is orders of magnitude greater
Than what you choose to remember and share.

Deliberate distortions will be found out.

Twice as Rich: Half as Wide

We have a different class of Martyrs out here:
Jed Smith, Alfred Packer, Narcissa and Marcus Whitman
The guy they had for lunch at Donner Pass.

I've always felt the U.S. of A. would be
Twice as rich if it were only half as wide.

Take out the useless tier of states starting in Arizona,
Rip up thru Utah and Nevada, Wyoming and Montana,
And the great northern stack from Texas to Dakota
All gone, all freed up, a ten bagger plus one.

Then one could travel from San Diego or LA,
Thru Santa Fe and on to New Orleans
Without all that intervening Apache desert of Texas and Arizona.

Or split from San Francisco thru Denver and on to Saint Louis,
Saying "no thanks" to Salt Lake "City," or imagine this, Nebraska.
The really northern route from Seattle to Minneapolis and Chicago,
Hold the Aryan Nations of Idaho, Yellowstone and the befuddle Sioux.

Who will miss the parts left out?
I like this place better already.

Substantial and Desire

Twenty-nine years ago on Sunday
Charles Olson died,
January the 10th, 1970.
I'd just come back from Boise
To hear Edward Smith preach
Who two months before in a trench coat
Had come with green seedless grapes and
A box of heavy chocolates
To redeem me from the psyche ward.

The hospitals of infirmity surround us.
I dig my ancestors' bones
Who got this far on nothing
More substantial than desire.

Life in Salt Lake City is at odds with theology.
Life always wins but theology hangs around
Like a bad joke in unused gravity with nothing to hold it down.

Edward has been gone again,
This time for eight years into the wilderness
Of disconnected phone numbers and undeliverable mail.

What does it mean to have a friend you can rarely find,
Who means so much and appears so little,
Whose mere understanding makes the day fairly swarm with meaning.

Come back and get me
Is a song sung through
An open heart.

I'm going through my Saturn's paces
Following the sun around
An unstable orbit.

Olson dead before I'd begun

To sink my teeth into the hard stuff
And come up clean and empty, Ishmaelian.

Winter wears
A skiff of ice frozen dew
Otherwise unnaturally warm.

"There's no more climate, it's all weather,"
So says Stephen Thomas
Archpoet of the new dead reckoning.

The mink relinquishes his fur bearing smile
Across the frozen beaver pond.
Silence is identical to the only thing you hear.

For all the effect America's going
To have on the world finally,
There might as well be total ocean
Between Tenerife and Taiwan.

Direct route to the orient discovered.
The Western Hemisphere is a mistake.

Poison Aire

Waking up alive is always a treat
Until you read the newspapers.

Yesterday off the coast of Coos Bay, Oregon,
The Coast Guard napalmed the *New Carissa* into fire,
A derelict Japanese oil tanker
Registered in and flying the flag
Of the Chicken Shit Fiction of Panama
To avoid national or international environmental laws
Which patently do not exist,
Before they torpedoed it to sink it and
Get the mess finally out of sight.

The air is not as thick as you might think.
It's only five miles deep
And more expendable than the water in the sea apparently.

Once we've released enough carbon and sulfur
Monoxide, dioxide, trioxide, try suicide into the air
We'll need gas masks just to walk to the store
In this nouveau Neptunian atmosphere
Already here in Mexico City with
Oxygen rejuvenation stations
Along every block of *La Reforma*.

The smart money is in oxygen futures,
Light weight tanks to strap on your back
For a stroll down the dead end streets of paradise.

The Weather Report: From the Front

There is no more climate,
It's all weather now
            Stephen Thomas

Low pressure north of here sucks the wind
Through the bare February branches of
Oak Beech and Maple making
Palouse Street hum and howl after Midnight.
Is this the way a river sounds underwater?

Warmth in winter, drenching rain
Drought in the farm belts
Unheard of barometric
Highs and lows
Cobble the climate into smithereens.

Every crop, every mouth, every strangled cry
Regardless of how hollywooded out with feigned indifference
Depends on the weather for its extensivity.
You won't be eating here again
With that fake aplomb you've become famous for.

Pity the starving children who can't get straight answers
From politicians made pale by the TV camera's red light.
We've taken the earth and the people who work it
For granted, for a ride, for long enough.
There is always room for more humility.

Outside the stars twinkle reminders
To the dark earth with its back turned
On the sun.
We giggle, we gaggle, we're ridiculous.
The solar winds of real change have begun to blow.

The Western Jet Stream

Normally the jet stream loops
Alternately North and South
Contributing to the creation of
Winter on the Blue Mountain face of
The Columbia Basin.

La Niña takes the kinks out of the jet stream.
Directly West to East it blows
Neither warm nor cold but full of rain
Relentlessly the branches of the barely dormant
Deciduous trees sway and break off.

Whoever thought I'd live long enough to say
"I miss Winter," and it's alternatively freezing cold
Chinook thaw with sunshine.
Even the fog has failed to form.
It's been one nameless season since October.

Whether the weather really matters or not
Is not a topic for an unfocused group of
Upstart primates walking upright
Shaking and holding hands on
A celestial isolation ward.

The fossil and geologic record isn't interested
In whether or not our bones get recorded.
It's pretty clear the climate
Has been all over the map.
Edgy wind wakes me any
Hour of the day or night,
Drives me over the edge.

Do you miss the climate
You're most prone to
Pray for deliverance from
Your inextricably mixed
Responsibility and irrelevance?

Cross Winds

Cross winds tip trees over
Breaking power lines, branches,
Drive storm clouds across Snoqualmie Pass
In steady unpredictable sequences
Where snow reigns and avalanches itself
Over unsuspecting illprepared uninformable
Inhabitants.

La Niña y El Niño
El Double El Diablo Spanish fraternal twins
Give a sexy whipsaw edge to unpredictable weather.

This is a job for Woden
Norse god of poetry war and weather.
War is a win lose or draw proposition.
Weather is a win win lose lose
Non-Aristotelian plunge
Into daily divergence with your flexibility intact.

No two days, no two snowflakes, no two poems or people
Are ever exactly alike
Nor will they brace themselves the same
Tossed about on the same cross winds.

In the American Way

Once poison became their practice
The American way went sideways systematically
From the adoption of the Bill of Rights to
The Battle at Wounded Knee
There was a lot of dead air on
Radio Free America.

History isn't news, nothing was being broadcast
Short of Hamilton's Assumption
That if I make all my friends rich
By palming their debts off on the unsuspecting
A permanently bitter class of interest payers
Can be cemented into the foundation.

The national debt is more extensive
Than will ever be paid in full or in part
Because the time value of money is designed
To rob you of your time by making
Money more valuable than work and
Leisure a luxury that had been normal in paradise.

Without money you are in the American way
To cyberspace where the production of
Even thinner air postpones the inevitable gasp of reality
Out to that translucent moment
When the energy bill exceeds the grasp
And rolling blackouts illuminate California.

A vacation from this nonsense is in order
To pay some obeisance to the laws of
Thermodynamics that really matter.
MTBE makes the gas burn clean
While it poisons the air above the driveways
In the American way.

The Silver Dollar Bar & Grill
for Bobcat Travis Catsull

Silver dollars went out of circulation even in the western mountains during the time of my flamboyant youth when I was in high disregard of the economic juggernaut bearing down on the disorganized world.

Silver dollars used to weight our jeans down and seemed to be worth no more than the silver certificates we used to call "dollar bills" in their treasury green that folded into our wallets and we thought the girls liked more.

Silver dollars have been replaced by federal reserve notes now called dollars to say nothing of Susan B. Anthony who carried this civilization on her back before they made an eight-sided quarter-sized *silver* dollar out of nickel to honor her.

If you think about it much, the standing liberty silver dollar in the form of a female figure against oppression might have honored her leadership of our struggle more.

Sacajewea carried her baby on her back in Idaho guiding Lewis and Clark. She looks over her shoulder at us now from a new gold colored *silver* dollar as we get set to rhapsodize two hundred years of uninterrupted plunder.

Over a hundred years ago "Free Silver" was the rallying cry of William Jennings Bryan, three-time presidential candidate of the outspent, out-lied, outright manipulated Democratic party of ordinary people.

Since we got tired of the upper Neolithic and banging one another over the head with handy stones when some bright man or woman spilled some tin into the copper we got to be Bronze aged and metallic.

From then on it's been round the clock war over the supply of metal easily divided into the hundred year war for this or the hundred year war for that but those are just handles for a continuous process that won't be contained or stopped.

Plutonium is the metal of choice whose supply must be controlled today Lest rogue states put it in their ice cream and concoct a sundae no one can disassemble Chernobyl wise as radiation leaks its secrets into the water of life.

Gallium Arsenide is the real metal to be hoarded, more like silicon than silicon itself in the speed with which it can relay messages.

Fiber optics replaced copper, paper replaced silver money, I dig down into my Mormon genes for the phrase which says one day a pound of wheat will be worth more than a pound of gold.

Just as paper money in the form of federal reserve notes drove metal out of circulation, bullshit poetry before a distracted audience can drive real poets crazy with its fraudulent success.

So what's the message at whatever speed I can concoct except love? Hippys were an outrage against the market because we reinvented the commune without ever having read Marx.

We began to cooperate between cities and over time, sharing food, housing, clothes and sex outside the boundaries of commerce.

We were correctly perceived as a threat and our style was appropriated. Wear some flowers in your hair *if you're going to San Francisco* and the culture was sold back to us at inflated prices along with the tiresome ten-year colonial war on the hapless Vietnamese.

The Hippys were crushed like many tribes before them and some began to ape the values of the over-class. They became Weathermen, Charles Manson's Family, The Symbionese Liberation Army, while Morning Star and other ranches of the soul fell into disrepair.

At Drop City near Trinidad in southern Colorado, 1971, it came home again to me one night In one of Fuckminister Buller's geodesic domes as I laughed out loud while some frustrated Neo-Hippy tried in vain to get his electronic music together so he could listen to the "Jimi Hendrix Experience" on his headphones.

Buckminster Fuller wrote a long dull poem on the subject of the Industrial Revolution. I don't know the history of the Hippys other than my own well enough to recite it. I know we were warm and beautiful once and were eaten whole by the American version of our remote Greek past.

I can still see the Latin rendition of that story in the somber aggravated tones of Goya's "Saturn Devouring His Sons."

I had this vision in Berkeley when I was too weak to do anything about it.

We were economic ciphers and cooperation was just another untaxed drug on a saturated market. It had to be suppressed in favor of the higher-end cooperation of the bankers and aristocrats.

Whatever else you and your generation are able to make of itself in your moment of time, you recognize intuitively your economic cipherhood as you plan to spook it out for a few weeks or months at Hewlett Packard's graveyard before you become the spent fuel and the entropic violation of the 2nd Law of Thermodynamics.

Didja know that HP twenty years ago bought many ranches in the mountains of Idaho in the valley on the river where I was spawned, disconnected by lava flows, earthquakes and waterfalls from anything I can get back to, to dodge some major taxes owning land that only loses money once you've forgotten how to love it.

Keep your brilliant head together in this disorganized confusion. You are always welcome here to rest or "pray for a few bucks hibernating in our one-truck town."

We have plenty of room and my interest in your well being and coping skills remains keen.

I Chinga Su Madré

I Chinga su madré's
A new kind of poem.

Could only in English
Be composed,
But you still got to understand
Spanish and Chinese
Or the metaphor will fail you.

A yoking of the sacred and profane

I Chinga su madré
Sets the limits
Like *mama mi huevos*
And *cao nide xing.*

We will surrender in Spanish to the Chinese.

La Niña

We have two seasons now:
Summer and six months of October
When the wind drives rain directly
East to west on a jet
Stream equidistantly south
Of the simple Arctic Circle.

Formerly the snow would fall and drift
On wind occasionally blowing
North to south when ice would
Form on top of water.

I miss fall much less spring
This missing winter of the human heart.
Who would have thought it mattered
How cold the ocean gets.

The Closed Sea

Ima Nanji Desu Ka?

What time is it? is a question you learn
Eventually in every foreign language you study.
The answers to it are readily changeable.
It's in fact one of the few questions you can ask
Over and over again
And get a different correct answer every time
Which makes it very useful to teach
People how to talk in unfamiliar tongues.

So what's so special about
Ima nanji desu ka?
Which is only the Japanese version
Of the universal question
What time is it?

In the *Ji Chu Han Yu Ke Ben*
Basic Chinese Reader
Students are not introduced to
Xianzai jidian zhong?
The Mandarin equivalent of
Ima nanji desu ka?
Or what time is it?
Until Lesson 21,
205 pages into the first book.

Amazing how much time has passed in laidback Chinese
Before it was deemed necessary
By the official Beijing Language Institute
To teach you how to tell time.

Which gets us back to
Ima nanji desu ka?
Which is the *first* sentence you learn in
Mizutani's widely used *Introduction to Modern Japanese*
Published by the *Japan Times*.

Shall we make too much of time?
What difference does it make to cultures
How they tell, divvy up and otherwise
Conceive of and use time?

For the Japanese it's always time
To be doing something beautiful.
Ima nanji desu ka?
It's time to get started.

Since the Japanese are always doing something with one another
And that itself is beautiful,
What ever is done is distributed in time.
It's critically important that everybody in the group
Participate in time and on time as if it mattered.

You are what you do
With the time that you have.

The Big Bang theory of language occurred
To distribute time,
To keep everything from happening
At the same time in the same place—
The linguistic purpose of the universe.

Escapen From English

To escape from English in Fukuoka
I read a Spanish grammar book
Written in Japanese.

En face translations of *Español* into *Nihongo*
Space my cadet mind out of its body.

This is the way to third position
Completely out of culture.

Who needs language anyway
Except to chat as if you cared
About the gruel of communication.

English drives its speakers centrifugally
Always away from the center of mass
Times velocity squared.

There is nothing at the center to get back to,
To say nothing of the fact that the center has moved
With force on asymmetrical time.

The escape velocity of English careens
Us in to traveling solo in a single direction
To start over somewhere else.

Outside of English and into my body I rocket.

Made in Japan

I should have and may still
Write a poem filled with tea ceremonies
Shinto Shrines and Sumo, Pachinko Parlors and sushi bars
Yakusa and castles, Geishas and kerosene,
But the only part of Japanese culture that really interested me
Was the culture itself, ie the language.

Skosh was a cheap WWII era Japanese import from *skoshi*
Meaning a little, a smidgen, give me a skosh.

All morphology is portable.
The Japanese imported every English word in that language and now
Mispronounce them as the *Gairaigo* part of their own lexicon.
How can I make it more obvious that I'm after big game
Than by saying: It is the syntax I import.

Just as it is Japanese syntax that keeps me carving
Up the perfect misunderstandings accepted as the norm,
It is English if/would flexibility that when added to
Chinese geographic and intentional superiority
Will get their bluff across.

The Japanese of course made off with half
The Chinese add-a-line writing system
For its decorative purposes and its
Homophonic disambiguative capacity.

The English took everything that wasn't nailed down
And much that was.
It hasn't done them any long term good nor will it.
English speakers have no style; They steal *things* for Christ sakes.

European modification of Chinese technology
Helped produce the renaissance,
But more credit is probably due to the spices from
The South Mollucan Islands as Europeans soured on the taste of
Mutton fat and wheat.

The Shrine on Half a Hill

(near the mouth off
the west side of *Nagara Gawa*
in the village of *Meinohama*)

The shrine on half a hill implies
The missing half was not
Holy enough.

Was shoveled off into the bay
And twice as much as might have been otherwise possible
Built on the resultant flatland.

Across the river and into the hill
Side now slammed tight with
Cement blown out of an electric gun.

I climbed up alongside
The fence to keep the faith-
Ful from falling off.

The *Kami* way
Not the Commy way
Destroy half to save half.

Each time we cut things in two by half
What we have left is diminished by half.
At this rate we'll never run out.

The shrine on half a hill.
The left half.
The other half left.

Acros Fukuoka

Acros Fukuoka is a far out building
In the middle of *Tien Jin* adjacent to the park and city hall.
You can get to the subway *chikatesu* station
From *Acros Fukuoka*.
It has a concert hall and many
Over priced and trendy shops and restaurants in the basement.

I often went to the *Kokusai Hiroba* on the 3rd floor
To the lending library for *Gaijins*
It has a hollow middle up through the spiraling atrium.

The best part was the back facing the park.
14 stories zigguratted up with plants on each one.
Acros Fukuoka the buildings are growing.
It resembled what the hanging gardens of Hammurabi
Must have looked like.

Acros Fukuoka sounds like an ode.
I walked in the night without fear through the shrines
Unlit as befits holy molecular
Palms, *torii*, bells of Shinto.
Take my hand, I'm deranged in paradise.

The Sea Hawk

The sea hawk perched on the concrete wave breaker
At the edge of *Hakata* Bay rightly regards me with suspicion
I cannot alleviate.

The Closing Sea

On the beach at *Katsurahama* imagine
You can see all the way out to California
And send a poem in a bottle
Across the choppy water
Beyond the enormous concrete jacks that break
The water in riprap fashion from carrying
The hand placed sand back into the sea.

Sakamoto Ryoma,
Built like a horse if his statue is accurate,
Came from *Kochi* in *Shikoku*
To help put the finishing touches on
The *Meji Ishin* or restoration.

Here in *Shikoku*
The fourth world of the Japanese
You could get the impression that Lafcadio Hearne
Never quite got it.

In the old days before Japan was united
By *Toyotomi Hideyoshi* and *Tokugawa Iyaseu,*
The Japanese like the Germans and everybody else
Made simple club and sword warfare on one another.

Immediately after the unification
With *Toyotomi* in the lead in western Japan
The first thing they did was invade Korea
With the ultimate intent of capturing Beijing.

No longer politically possible to project hostilitics on one another
This 1592 up thrust of hostilities
Was directed outside of Japan at the closest target,
The linguistic kissing cousins,
The Koreans.
They never got to let alone beyond
The Yalu River.

The projection of hostilities is difficult to master
Before being assimilated
And *Toyotomi* was as slow a learner as other possessors of power.
He invaded Korea yet again in 1598,
Only getting half as far before the light and his death
Began to dawn upon him.

Tokugawa holed up in *Edo* in Eastern Japan on the *Kanto* plain,
—Japanese school children call these guys
Who pissed in unison on the pass at their initial victory in 1591,
"The two *pissoirs* of the *Kanto* Plain,"—
Tired of all the western adventuring.
He'd imagined a way to distribute and internalize
The prevailing hostility.

To carry out his plan his forces defeated
Those supporting *Toyotomi* in 1600 at
The Battle of *Sekigahara.*

Welcome to the *Edo Jidai* or *Tokugawa Jidai*
Which lasted from 1600 to 1868, 268 years,
Almost exactly the average length of a Chinese dynasty.
For 14 generations *Tokugawa* and his primarily literal progeny
Ruled Japan from *Tokyo*, the Eastern Capitol, or *Edo*
By keeping every *Daimyo's* wife and children
Under house arrest in *Edo* while
The *Daimyos* were required to spend
Half of each year on their *Daimyo*
And half in *Tokyo* with their families.

The possibilities of revolt were scant under these circumstances,
Never mind for the time being, the 47 *Ronin*,
And *Tokugawa* had the good sense to
Eliminate the Catholic Christian,
Read Spanish and Portuguese colonial influence,
Primarily from *Kyushu* and the area around *Nagasaki* because

They lacked "affinity" in his words and people who lack affinity are
Very difficult to estimate.

Sakamoto Ryoma, in league with many especially
The *Satsuma* clan from *Kagoshima,*
Toppled the *Tokugawans* and began the *Meji Ishin.*

Once the *Mejis* got their bearings
And learned how other people did it,
After they defeated the Russians in
The Russia-Japanese War of 1904,
Unlike the British whose navy controlled
The key points of commerce,
The Japanese Co-Prosperity Sphere
Began taking Korea and China
County by county, province by province
In a demonstration case of the long term limitations of
Linguistic concrete sequentialism.

Anybody who doesn't know Japanese
And how their social structure
Which is very firm,
Can support a social organization
Which can be whatever and as flexible as it has to be
Because the structure is composed of vertices,
—Imagine a bundle of *soba* noodles—
Each independent but tied to hang together at the middle,
Will have difficulty understanding how responsibility is diffused
Up and down the vertice but not across
From one noodle to another.

So the *Kwantung* Army
More or less independently engineered
The *Mukden* Incident and took the *Liaodong Bandao,*
The peninsula of *Dalian,*
Which led directly in English speak,
From one thing to another,

From the Bombing of the civilian population of *Shanghai*
[Four years before the European Fascists bombed *Guernica*]
Only 800 kilometers southwest of *Fukuoka,*
To the Rape of *Nanjing,* to the bombing of *Corregidor*
And the "surprise" attack on Pearl Harbor,
To the Battle of the Coral Sea,
The Battle of Midway,
The Battle for *Saipan,*
And finally the atomic bombing of
Hiroshima and *Nagasaki.*

Japanese can claim with a straight face
To have been victimized by their own *Kwantung* Army
Even though those people speaking a
Subject Verb Object language like *Zhongguo Hua* or English
Aren't buying it.

Japanese has the terminal verb
Which throws the subjects and the objects for a loop
Since circumstances are constantly changing,
They've changed before I get to the end
Of a well made Japanese sentence
And in which I have changed my mind
Along the pathway of morphemes
Until I do whatever I have to do
To keep the upper hand.

Because Japanese language
To be spoken properly has to first locate
Every speaker and receiver of speech
Somewhere on the vertice,
Either up or down and
Preferably below in the great *Keigo* of social looking down the nose at
"Look out everybody below."

2

Many of my most endearing moments
Have been spent enthralled in conversation
With a few of the world's great psychiatrists:

Alexander Lowen, author of dozens of books,
Available in many of languages,
The Betrayal of the Body, Bioenergetics,
The man who applied and extended the fruitful insight of
Wilhelm Reich;

H..C. Tien, of an old *Beijing* family and Lansing, Michigan,
Founder of the *Pinxxiee* system of alphabetizing the Chinese radicals
To electronify ideographic languages;

Doi Takeo, author of among other fine works,
Amae No Kozo and *Omote To Ura,*
The Freud of Japan if there is such a thing
Who lived in *Tokyo* through the Earthquake of 1923 as a child,
And through the fire bombing of *Tokyo* by the American Air Force in
World War II as a recent graduate of *Todai, Tokyo Dai Gakkue.*
Who has seen *Tokyo* destroyed and rebuilt twice in his lifetime,
Still with a twinkle in his and their indomitable eye.

The titles of Doi's books cited above read respectively as
The Structure of Dependent Love,
Although it is translated as *The Anatomy of Self,*
And *Front and Back.*

Lowen's greatest work,
The Physical Dynamics of Character Structure,
Got retitled for the popular market as
The Language of the Body.

What is it our systems of publishing and therefore
Systems of public understanding have in these two instances with
A chary wariness of "structure?"

They seek to eliminate the physical dynamic.
They have no use for the structure of love.

Character is structure under pressure.
They think they can take the bones from the body,
Remove the pressure of pleasure
To make the skeleton and the body dance alone.

Structure is the one thing people have to understand.
Nothing will happen that is not supported by structure.
Certain fascist structures are designed to keep
Anybody from succeeding.
This calls into being an alternative structure
A revolution in language
Leading to peace and freedom
Leaving dead and ineffective people
Atop their toppling structures.
As the Greek Gods used to say
"If people stop believing in us we're dead."

Long live the dead
Who hang on like recrudescent viruses
Longing to be brought back to life
But will have no life in the lands of the living.

3
I catch the bus back to *Kochi*
Saying goodbye to *Katsurahama*
Watching the woman in waders plant
The other half of her rice paddy
Out the window in *Shikoku*
Far enough South to harvest
Two crops per year.

Pacific Person

What do you suppose *Tokugawa* meant
When he wrote to the King of Spain about
The Spaniards and the Portuguese
Christians disturbing the culture in *Kyushu*
Before he crucified some of them and
Threw the rest of them out:
"You have no affinity
And people without affinity are
Very difficult to estimate."

Chinese and English Rejoicing at the Size of Japan

Everyday
Unnoticed even by satellites
That ensnare the globe continuously
Shooting geosynchronous photographs
Of everything that moves
And much that remains stationary

More than a billion Chinese
And 3-4 hundred million more or less Americans
Fall to their knees and prostrate themselves
Or give thanks in other less detectable ways
That the four major and many minor
Islands of Japan
Aren't any larger in the aggregate
Than the surface of the state of Montana.

All Japanese history is an elaboration of
The relationship between people and fish.

Honda, Hondu, Hondo

In my youth not quite fresh out of college I worked
For the man who had Honda Franchise Number One,
Honda of Washington assigned in 1959.

Honda Sochiro made an assault
On the American motorcycle business
And on his way played a big part
At putting to bed the sneer in the phrase
"Made in Japan."

Sochiro came to LA one day and was aghast, appalled and horrified
At the way American bikers looked on their Harley Davidsons,
Your basic Hell's Angel black leather jacket and pants
With fake silver rivets and fringed decals,
Bandannas, tattoos and chrome sissy bars to hold up
The female of the species.

"You meet the nicest people on a Honda"
Was his rejoinder as the bright red, toy like Honda 90s, 250s, 650s
        and beyond
Became staple nutpick rattlers of a broad array of American streets.

A honda could also be
The metal eye at one end of a lariat
Through which the other end is passed to form
A running noose.

Hondo is a low lying Spanish arroyo
In the Southwest and Mexico where kids on dirt bikes
Fly their Hondas up through the hondos,
Snakes and scorpions look out.

Hondu is whatcha do when you can't do
Anything else.
Honda, hondu, hondo, *Hoonda*.

2

Honda Sochiro built the world's most successful motorcycle company
After Harley Davidson of Ohio,
And brought on a succession of Yamahas, Suzukis, and Kawasakis
       from Japan,
Bultacos from Spain, Moto Guzzis from Italy and a two wheeled
       revolution.

Honda wanted to build cars.
He was told by the Ministry of Trade and Industry
The venerable *Tsushosangyosho*,
Essentially to get lost.

MITI said we want there to be
Three manufacturers of Japanese automobiles:
Toyota, Nissan and Mazda.
I don't see Honda on that list, do you?

You may have gotten taken in by the phrase "Japan Inc."
But if Japan Inc. doesn't want you in their Inc.
You're expected to go away because after all
Japan is nothing if not a top down vertical hierarchy filled
With a hundred million gleaming obsequious souls.

Our man Honda said "Nuts to you, Japan Inc."
Because he had cash flow sufficient from his motorcycle business
To be his own
Keiretsu, Zaibatsu and bank.

Local gold, local Yen
Locus stupendi Honda brought out
In those waning days of the middle late sixties
The first Honda automobile for sale in North America.

The guffaws went on all night.
It was a cabover roller skate,
Two motorcycles yoked together with a front and rear axle.

Its serious problems were almost beyond tally.
An American man of average size could barely squeeze in.

But Honda was a serious man and listened politely as most geniuses do
To his most severe critics,
Because if you have confidence they are the only people
Who can tell you what you really need to know,
And out of the factory each year came
A new, improved and better Honda.

As the improvements accumulated in the continuous improvement
        mode
Endemic to Japanese yearning for perfection,
By 1985, a mere twenty years later,
Out came Honda as car of the year,
A better engineered vehicle than Mercedes-Benz
Who'd been at it by that time for nearly a century.

Honda did it without help, with want to power,
To the astonishment of his Japanese detractors who
Resisted and impeded him in his own words,
"Every step of the way."

Japan may be a bundle of *soba* noodles
Of uniform size, consistency and nutritious effect.
In fact the most interesting Japanese
Are men like Honda, an oxymoronic phrase,
For Honda was truly *sui generis*,
Who cut at perpendicular angles
Directly across the grain.

You'll see more of it in the best Sumo wrestlers and in the
Most effective Japanese politician since World War Two,
Tanaka Kakuei.

Perpendicular to the Noodle

The best Japanese go cross grain.
To the *Keigo* tradition of honorific language
Begetting honorific behavior
They give the American equivalent of
The green weenie bird.

Honda and *Tanaka* in our time,
Automobiles and politics,
Chewed the system up and spit it out,
Made it do
What they had in mind.

Remember the great all purpose Japanese verbs:
Kuru and *Suru*
To come and to do.

Any nominal on earth can be turned
Into a Japanese to do verb,
Shi masen desu taka?

The great Japanese question:
Kima shimastaka?
What did you come here to do?

Nakasendo

I'm on the road, the royal road, the Japanese equivalent of
    El Camino Real,
On foot and ecstatic all day.
I came here early this morning on the train,
From *Matsumoto*, although I passed through yesterday admiring
The river valley at *Kiso Fukushima*, went on all the way to *Nagano*
To check it out. I knew I wouldn't be back for the Olympics.
We're in the Japanese Alps.
The valley at *Nagano* reminded me of the Kittitas Valley in
    central Washington
Where Mount Stewart rose over Ellensburg as seen from
    Manastash Ridge.

I got back to *Nagiso Eki* in plenty of time to catch the bus.
So I crossed and
Recrossed the river on foot on a suspension bridge,
Admiring the cherry blossoms
Wishing I knew Japanese better to deepen the flirt with the clerk.

I had the good sense to take the bus all the way to the top of
    Magome Toge,
The pass out of the valley on this drainage, so that I could walk
    the 20 miles back
To the station downhill.
Every joyful step I effuse.
I've never felt more like me.

I pass a drinking station, more like a watering trough.
I'm wearing tennis shoes.
The road is dusty.
This is the old way from *Kyoto* to *Tokyo* during *Tokugawa Jidai.*
I'm tracing steps samurai took both ways, in triumph and disaster.
I could be one of the 47 *Ronin.*
Instead I'm one of the 15 who took a powder.
Who had more important things to do than patronize a dead tradition.

At the dimorphic water falls there is a slight dip in my
	ecstatic condition.
I encounter the uniformed cackle of Japanese high school students on
	an outing.
It is their world.
The students who are as numerous at shrines and tourist attractions
	as tourists
Act like well trained zoo animals. Cultured oysters or is it pearls.

Through the wooden walled town of *Tsumago,* the object of my desire,
Much later in the afternoon, it could be 160 years earlier.
I expect *Toshiro Mifune*
To materialize around any corner. Beautiful gardens.

I pass an irresistible uphill mistake:
The road to the top of a peak way down the valley
That leads to a stupendous view.
I ascend to admire the pass shimmering
Through the haze and put the kibosh on my downhill swing.
19th century high tech meant higher ground, meant a view
Of enemy movement.
I exult enemyless and crash hard back at the hostel,
Talking half the night in Japanese to three working guys
Who correct my mistakes endlessly, good naturedly,
	after the public bath,
The walk around *Matsumoto Jo,*
The beautiful black castle with the hidden floor.

The road through the middle opens at both ends.
I take this walk over and over again.
I'll never be able to retrace a single step.
I think of *Miyazawa* and *Suguwara,* my other
More direct Japanese friends.
I will never leave these moments.
The ambient air
I intentionally disturb.
I wish I'd bought a larger carp flag.

Walk Across *Tokyo*

for *Doi Takeo* and *Takahashi Kenji*

When I walk across *Tokyo* I'm falling in love
Every step of the descending way
Through the Imperial Palace grounds
On my way back from a visit with *Doi Takeo*.
I admire the 100 foot high angled basalt walls
Of the moats surrounding this palace.
I'm going to cruise the gleaming banks
Of *Ote* and *Muromachi*
As I head for *Tokyo Eki*
And the return train ride back to
Emily and Natalie at *Miki* and *Yuroko's* house in *Kamakura.*

Before the Bubble Economy popped
The *Bubberu Keizai* had the palace grounds
On the real estate assessment books as being worth more
Than the dwindled dominion of Canada.

They were mistaken as to what constitutes
Consolidates and contributes to wealth in concentration,
In the extension of credit under which
There was no value added.

Takahashi Kun and his friends came on the train
All the way from *Yokohama*
To take me out to *Tonkatsu* dinner,
Breaded pork loin with sauce and finely shredded cabbage.
Later we went on *Yo Hanami,*
Flower viewing at night
And threaded our way through drunken *salarimen,*
Bureaucrats and their wives strung out for miles
Along the strip of blooming cherry trees
That rims the western edge of the palace grounds
On cardboard spreads to keep the dewy grass
Off their good and *saked*-up clothes.

Later we walked in front of the *Kokkai* or Diet Building,

Imposing in the dark as we changed taxies
And I returned to *Aoyama*.

Are the neighborhoods of *Tokyo* all interesting to me
Simply for their exotic appeal as they surround
This still awesome economic engine?
The Japanese language insists on refinement,
It's why they polish the nutrition off of rice
And look askance on barbarians like myself
Who insist on eating *Genmai* or brown rice.

They've polished the crime right off the streets
And institutionalized it in *Okurasho*, the Ministry of Finance.
In Japan the polite mugging begins
The moment you get your passport and visa.
Individuals aren't allowed to hoard money here
The way the crooks at the top of the English and American systems do.

It's taxed out from under them and endlessly recycled
In a beautiful velocity that permits the system
To continue delivering goods and services
In the teeth of the terrible Depression, or *Fukkyo*.

If you walked a few blocks in New York at night
Before the rectitude reign of Don Guiliani
You'd want a rifle butt to knock the teeth out of
Muggers as they case your joints in the bankrupt community
That used to be called America.

Doi Takeo with a twinkle in his 76 year-old eye
Has seen it all come and go.
He was a child when the *Kanto* Earthquake
Knocked *Tokyo* to the ground in rubble in 1923.
He was a young graduate of *Todai* in 1945
When Curtis LeMay and the American Army Air force
Burned *Tokyo* to the ground with firebombs,
A devastation practically as complete as

Dubiously did in *Hiroshima*
Via the Enola Gay.

In other words *Doi* has seen
Tokyo destroyed and rebuilt twice in his lifetime.
Would such demonstrated resilience inspire faith or what
In this brilliant psychiatrist, thinker and writer.

Japanese faith is not in real estate.
It is in the continuously refining impulse of
The well-made Japanese sentence.

The most common verbs in English are
To be and to have.
The basic question in English is
And we hear it and ask it of each other all the time,
Where are you and what have you got?

The most common verbs in Japanese are
Kuru and *Suru* or
To come and to do respectively.
In fact you can turn
Any Japanese nominal
Which really means any nominal on earth
Through the imported loan word process of *Gairaigo*,
Into a verb by adding suru to the end of it,
The not quite equivalent of the "do" insertion in English.

The upshot of this verbal dexterity is,
With the Japanese verb in the terminal position in
The subject object verb distribution of Japanese syntax,
The common question in Japanese becomes,
What did you come here to do?

I come here to do wa diddy,
To do the time I have left proud,
To share what I know with people who can use it.

The Great English Verbs

The great English verbs
To be and to have
Reduce life to the basic question:
Where are you and what have you got?

Which means they are about
Position and possession.
You must be strong if you
Would keep your balance.

The great Japanese verbs
Kuru and *suru*
To come and to do
Render Japanese interrogative life as
What did you come here to do?

Which means they are about
Aggression and activity,
The ability and intention to move toward
The things you want with style.

What happens when we blend
Any or all four of these together in
Dynamic juxtaposition?

To be and to do
Something beautiful
Where I am
With what I've got
I've got to get there first.

Come where we are to have
Something to do.
What nonverbal life would be like
We can't even imagine.

Okurasho and the Velocity of Money

In downtown *Tokyo* where the Ministry
Of Finance still stands,
The venerable *Okruasho*,
Where if the men in a single building could be called
The bag men of *Nihon* they would be.

From here and in its companion parts of
Nichigin, the national bank,
Is where *beaucoup Yen* is
Circulated from,

At half a percent now in the *Fukkyo* that started
When *Nichigin* raised interest rates
In the final week of 1989
And put the prick to the *Bubberu Keizai*
Elsewhere known as the Bubble Economy.

It took the better part of eight years for this deflation,
The credit mobile of imagination,
To get back to the United States
From which it sprang with the Plaza Accords of 1985.

If money is only worth half a percent
It means its time value has been removed.
It means there is nothing you can do with the money
That will make it worth any more than it is
The moment I hand it to you.

You've got to eat a lot of value added
For which you'll never be compensated
Just to keep the money in circulation
Let alone to have anything to show for it.

And the heroic Japanese have been doing just that,
Keeping their economy going by velocitizing money through it.
Never mind the *Jusen Mondai* and the crude facts

That most of the *Yen* 1300 trillion in bad loans
Eventually filtered down to the *Yakusa*
(If they didn't originate there)
Because the *Yakusa* traditionally do the dirty work.

Not the work reserved for the *Burakumin,*
The dead hides and animals of Japan's unmentionable untouchables,
But the dirty work of prostitution, gambling
And now as if it weren't dirty enough already,
Loans secured by non-performing real estate.

You don't foreclose on a *Yakusa* held loan
Unless you're planning to hang yourself
In your girlfriend's underwear on Monday,
Because the *Yakusa* are family
And families try to work their economic differences out peaceably.

Okurasho, which only has the combined functions of the
IRS, the SEC, the Federal Reserve Bank,
The Secretary of the Treasury, the White House and
Congressional Offices of
Management and Budget, plus the committee chair functions
From both houses of Congress of Finance, Appropriations, and
Ways and Means,
All under one roof with a single minister,
Could truthfully be said to control the Japanese economy.

The Bag Man of *Tokyo*
Is really a greystone building
Where the budgets are written and sent
To the Diet for ratification.

A *Fukkyo* is a depression,
A superabundance of capacity,
As differentiated from a recession
Which is a superabundance of inventory.

Inventory can be melted away,
Used and consumed.
Capacity has to be absorbed by end users with means.
Getting the Japanese economy expanding again
Or "growing our economy" in Bill Clinton's phrase
Is the only thing that can end a Depression,
But there are no markets demonstrating effective demand.
For what, more cars?

The underpaid Nike and other factory workers
In Indonesia and elsewhere
Aren't being paid enough to amortize the loans
From the corrupt-feigning generosity-first world.
It has been done in the past 50 years at the expense
Of the environment and labor, the poisoned air and water.

Zero Pronoun

Zero Pronoun
No relation to Zero Mostel
Except they have the same first name
Allows freedom of expression
Sans accolade.

For instance if I say
Bu zhi dao, bu dong
It's clear in Mandarin that it's me
Who doesn't know or understand
Without saying "Wo," (whoa).

In English far too many zeros
Keep their pronouns intact:
I, you, me, they, them, us, her, him, who
Anything except responsibility
Any zero will do.

The Japanese had to invent "Watashi"
And use the *Hanzi* for personal and private
In order to translate English
With its prevalent "I"s.

As for me
Watashi wa
I'm having none of it.

The Greeks didn't have
What the Chinese and Japanese didn't need.
Sounds like a perfect opportunity
For some international trade.

Make nothing happen
In a lot of places at once.

Japolish

For the first time in my history with DOS
A file name turns exactly into the title of the work.
Praise Gates. Praise doors. Praise windows.

Praise the Japanese who polish
Their verbs until you can't detect the motion.
Isn't that what a verb is all about?
An all purpose motion detector in a sea of calm?
The verbal equivalent of binocular envisioned eyes.

Japolish that verb for me would you please.
Use the glue that fuses Japanese and English.
Make words up from scratch.

I don't need permission to boost morphological elements,
The way language gives you a license to steal.
J. Bracken Lee,
No longer extant Mayor of Salt Lake City and
Governor of Utah, once said, in public,
"Being an attorney is like having a license to steal."

The Utah Bar Association upbraided him and
Demanded an apology.
Brack Lee did not back down; he repeated himself:
"Being an attorney is like having a license to steal."

Never mind shooting the lawyers on Shakespeare's sayso.
Language is a license to steal.
A little verb here, an adjective there,
Pretty soon you're making sense.

Whose words are they anyway?
Or were they, since they're mine now.
Every scrap of morphology is up for grabs.

Stealing syntax on the other hand
Now that could be a capitol crime,
More alert than a Promethean Coyote boosting fire.

A little polite Japanese insincerity
Shotgunned to the notion that
By the time you come to the end of the sentence
The head of the sentence has morphed so far into the past
It no longer means what you started to say, so *Keredomo*
And away you go with newly reflected meaning constantly
Talking about it although
It's already over.

EDP, 1968

[Electronic Data Processing]
ie computer center
IBM 360 mainframes
super fast adding machines

Bill Shimazu
#2 in command
#1 in control
Walked with a kitch in his getalong.

Nevertheless
He consistently in the lunch room
Removed the shell of a hard boiled egg
In a single piece.

Dynamic Sentence Sing

I mangle Standard American English
As often as the other guy
With relish as my preference inclines
Toward Japanese syntaxelizing
Of dynamic English phrasal verbs to wit:

A well made Japanese sentence ends with a verb
If it ever ends at all.
Keredomo or *deskedo*
Which follows many Japanese sentences
Is the but leading to the next phase of the thought.

Nothing ever stops in this process
Like it's apt to do in an English sentence.
Subject verb object end of story
Finished product saying
Buy sell store me and don't ask

About the details
The process which attempts to get at
The dynamic slap in the static.

Future Tense on Pacific Rim

Future Tense on Pacific Rim
Is how the headlines all will read
Since it will be conducted in English
With Japanese syntax
Over Chinese food.

There's more to this than clever jibes.
Everyone is going to have to give
Up something indispensable.
Control to start with will get out of control.
Especially on the English side who will start shooting.

The Japanese will chafe since syntax is not their favorite thing.
Honorific language sorting people into classes is.

The Chinese will finally lose their identity
In the witness protection program
Having kiped all the software books and music
With the radioactive hotware
They'll be back in the kitchen
Conducting the economy
As a feast of fried brains.

With no guns or class
Henry Kissinger will huddle with *Tanaka's* ghost,
Subject: Where did we go wrong?

You'd think America could do better
Across the yard wide Atlantic Ocean
Than this endless parade of European refugees
At the titular head of their so-called State Department.
No mention here of Zbigniew Brezenski.

And then the little things: Korean kimchee, Thai sex,
Indonesian peanut butter, disguised as salad dressing
With the puckered ass of hatchery salmon
To kiss on the side.

Retailing Poetry

On the top floor of the *Daimaru Depato* store
In the city of *Fukuoka's Tien Jin* commercial district
For at least a week during the month of April, 1996,
Half of the top floor gallery space
Was given over to a meticulous display
Of the holographs, implements and artifacts pertinent to
The 100th birthday celebration of the life and times of
The reclusive Buddhist poet, *Miyazawa Kenji.*

For weeks beforehand posters even larger by twice
Than those used in the United States to advertise movies
Were affixed to the sides of buildings, *Chikatetsu* stations,
And smaller versions were everywhere.

I love *Miyazawa's* poetry
For its direct elaborated simplicity,
Its compassion and commitment.

To see the hoes he worked the garden soil with,
His art work filled with the vibrant wonder of a child.
The collected works in many versions and several individual volumes
At the outrageous prices the Japanese economic system has become
        famous for,
Fairly flying off the stacks into the bags of
Housewives, *salarimen*, and students,
Thrilled me beyond the bone.

For I can say utterly without fear of contradiction
As the flat gold light of morning illuminates
The underside of the begonia's serrated leaves,
That such a scene has never nor will ever
Take place anywhere within the borders of these
Confining dis-United States.

Hating poetry as most Americans do,
And denying that it has any power,

Is after all only the hatred and denial
Of their own sweet tender feelings
Which Americans suppress as a military obligation
In favor of displaying their own crude Ice Age chilled aggression.

Buying no more books myself I still salute
The wan *Miyazawa* working, content to labor
In a minor village in the north of *Tohoku,*
Loved by now by housewives, *salarimen,* and students alike.
Retailing poetry, retailing feelings, retelling dreams.

Suguwara at Tenmangu

Suguwara at Tenmangu,
Sugi wa, you are sugi wa desu,
No doubt about it, next in English,
Next in Japanese, next in Nihongo,
First in the hearts of your children,
Especially the two of twenty three
You brought with you from Kyoto
Fourteen hundred kilometres away
On your way into permanent exile.

Dazaifu is a disarming place to die,
Charming administrative capitol of Kyushu
For five hundred years during Heian Jidai,
Now swarming with tourists and uniformed school children.
You haunt the heart shaped pond,
Who only lived here two years until you succumbed,
To age, to exile, to a badly broken heart.

What does it mean to have been the Minister of the Right?
Not the Minister of the Left?
Politics are the bane of poetry.
They threw you out of Kyoto.
You wrote late T'ang Shi, Tang Dynasty poetry in
Hanzi with a Japanese accent in the Heian Jidai in 966.

In my hanami memory on the steeply arched bridge
Of the flying plum alongside the water
That flew with you all the way from Kyoto to land
By the heart shaped poet's pond I say

I've been in exile all my life
And send this poem over backwards to you
A thousand years through time
As if it were tomorrow and we were together again
At last for the first time.

Full Moon Over *Meinohama*

There's a full moon over *Meinohama*
Where I'm certain that it's shining on who
Ever looks up and needs it the most
Westerly over *Nokonoshima* towards *Shanghai.*

Meinohama means my neice's beach
Where the subway rattles out from under *Fukuoka*
Before the trains trundle down the coast of *Kyushu*
To the 100 square foot weeping wisteria on the way to *Karatsu Jo*

Night comes to the castle at *Karatsu* and I'm reflected
In the plate glass windows of the *Sumitomo Ginko*
By the banks combination security/greeter
On the street level heart of *Tien Jin.*

The last train stops at Midnight.
The drunken *salarimen*
Coast on a sea of *saké.*
Jump start the poet's heart.

Giggling girls and taciturn guys
Uniformly behave.
Except for the green-haired skateboarders
Cluttering up the stairways at *Tien Jin.*

If I ever go back to *Fukuoka*
To my *Sanchomei* neighborhood in *Meinohama*
I'll follow the *Nagara Gawa*
All the way up the mountain to its source.

Japan's picturesque-icity
Fisherman *Nogamis* in a field of god.

Typhoon *Ju Yon Go*

The typhoon brought the tide in with it
Clear up to the curb on the *Nagara* River
Fifty feet from my front door.

It's been raining steadily
Since the last typhoon *Ju Ni Go.*
Ju San Go must have blew in and out
Outside of my cognition.

What happens when the tide inundates the street?

I've battened down the hatches
Slid the shutters from their casings
Over the windows, loaded up on *Genmai* (brown rice)
And other forms of easily fixed nutritious food.

When the weather comes to wash our tracks away
And there will be no witnesses left in this protection program
There will still be the sea and the shore.

The full moon over *Meinohama*
Will make the spinning top of the typhoon shine.

I Want to Go Back to *Nokonoshima*

I want to go back to *Nokonoshima*
And ride our bikes all the way around the island again.

I want to go back to *Katsurahama* and imagine
A poem in a bottle on its way to California.

I want to go back to *Tsumago* and pretend
I'm in 19th century Japan again.

I want to go back to *Ikedasans*
And climb the hill to look over
The straits of *Shimonoseki.*

I want to go back to the *Aoyama Ryoien*
And have that Japanese conversation again
With the old lady at dawn in the cemetery,
The young men still drinking
Cold beer and *saké* on the cardboard ground during *Hanami.*

I am not afraid to come out of my language.

Searching for *Mitsuhiro*
(*Mitsuhirosan o sagashite imasu*)

Mitsuhiro Tanaka San and *Kenji Takahashi San*
From *Yamate* High School in *Yokohama*
Spent two weeks with our family
Last year in April on cultural exchange.

Among the many presents they gave Natalie
Were two small cotton bears
Which she named after them.

Walking on the western shore of Wallowa Lake
During a break in the Fishtrap Writer's Conference
Natalie fell asleep in my backpack and let go of,
Lost *Mitsuhiro* as he fell from her relaxed hand.

Searching for *Mitsuhiro*
By backtracking the route
Served only to remind me of all the other
Mitsuhiros I've lost and how excited I had been
To have two, however temporarily,
Young Japanese "sons" in my house.

I'm told there is a tradition on Children's Day
In *Kyoto* when the parents of aborted and miscarried fetuses
Visit the temple to light the candles and bless the little Buddhas,
Bibbed or aproned and made of stone,
That they've enshrined to honor them.

The musical poet Bill Shively said,
Moved by attending such a ceremony and
Observing the love lavished on it,
"The unborn children are doing ok."

I draw comfort from the saving grace
Of being father to three beautiful daughters,
One more perhaps than the law, traditions, or
Some people's economics will allow
Me to be made rich beyond comprehension and
Forever humbled in their love.

Even as I go on Searching for *Mitsuhiro*
(Mitsuhirosan o sagashite imasu)
And find myself looking
Into the eyes and faces of every other young man or boy
I see or meet for clues to what being the father
Of a living son would be like, (Ghepetto)
Bringing those feelings to the surface of a
Gut wrenching complexity one more time.

I see again also the faces and feel the hands and
Cherish the love and affection bestowed upon me
By the necessarily nameless young women who went on
To abortions and miscarriages after spending some
Good times in my arms.
I dissipate into an invisible cloud of
Helpless shame and embarrassment.

Might one of them been my son?
Which I'll never have as I go on
Searching for *Mitsuhiro* (*San o sagashite imasu*)
In my memory and imagination,
Finding only fragments of my self in failed relationships
Still lost with a small cotton bear
Curled up by the trail and dimly reflected
In the faces of the dozens of young men and boys I help
Us to understand all of our children are
All of our children
And deserve our undivided attention and
Unconditional love.
Mitsuhiro san o sagashite imasu.

Remapping *Fukuoka*

On the evening beach at *Momochihama*
The red sun sets behind *Nokonoshima,*
Looking more like Jupiter without the eye
Through 500 miles of virtual pollution
Unchecked between here and *Shanghai.*

The aerial photograph in the children's museum,
Taken in *Showa* 33 or 1958,
Shows water where the new half of
Fukuoka's been built on landfill
Packed onto sea life at the edge of
A shrinking man made bay.

Evidence of many crimes are displayed
As Ann, Emily, Natalie and I
Walk the board walk licking over priced ice cream
Beneath the *Fukuoka* Tower.

The translucent blue tower
Is a not quite empty shell
With an electronic top.
An erector set erection of reflective glass,
A rectangular blue bottle fly,
With a high priced elevator ride
To somewhere beneath the top.

From the 35th floor of the Sea Hawk Hotel,
You can see the growth of the beautiful city in 6 directions,
Over the land, up into the air, across the sea,
Everywhere except the underground maze
Of shopping malls and subway grid.

The rambling lamentations of an ungrateful poet
Cannot redeem the dead air,
The polluted sea, the political cunning,
The fishy food, the insincere apologies,
The streets without and beyond name or number.

Driving the Demons — *Onisube at Dazaifu*

I re-read the map. The festival is on a flat space. South and higher up than the amusement park. Walk past some *Soba* shops. I have a bowl. The arena is fenced off and flood lit. A platform of loud speakers and a gate on one end. A two story building on the other with new wooden panels in front and ½ way down each side. I take a position up an incline at the corner steel fence post, erected to hold the crowd on the hill. Eventually the entire ground is filled with spectators including the entire other side of the arrangement. The arena is perhaps ½ acre.

Much *mamo naku*. In front of the building on the left side are bundles of rice straw stacked chest high. On the right side are coniferous boughs. The bullfinch exchange began at 7. By 7:30 I went to the *Onisuge*. By 8 first group of men came in, green *gis*, white headbands, chanting and running around behind the building carrying torches, unlit, on bamboo poles, 3 times around the building. Then they sat the torches along the fence nearest to me and we waited.

8:15: A group of mostly children, boys?, came in chanting and also running around. Some wore maroon, some wore green. They carried signs, white flappers on poles, Shamrocks on one side, the *kanji* for Destiny and something else on the other. They then left the arena and took up positions on the east side.

8:30: 3rd group 60-80 men with charcoal blackened faces, white cloth wrapped around their heads and braided antenna like horns protruding about 2 feet in front of them carrying a huge log and 20-30 placards such as the boys had, 3 times around. They laid the log in front of the building.

8:45: 30 men came in green *gis* carrying 3 12-15 foot long bundles of bamboo on fire at rear end. 3 times around the arena, behind the building, whooping, and then they stood the 3 burning bundles up on unlit end at north side of arena.

9:00: The moon came out. The maroon contingent moved the rice straw and pine bundles and form them into a bier or windrow, pulling the rice apart and winding up with a hedge 6 feet high of mixed rice and pine. It was soaked down with kerosene. Some Gold *gis* come in with lanterns on sticks. I think some of these men went into the building from the back. For a while I couldn't tell the demons from the priests. One priestly type came out the front of the building as two door panels were removed, chanting, and waving a lantern in the 10 foot area between the building and the fire row.

9:15: As the fire was lit the maroon contingent picked up their placards and began to fan the fire and smoke toward the building. Loud pounding could be heard inside the building as men inside with huge wooden mallets knocked the new wood off the walls into splinters. The fire leaped 10-15 feet in the air, little black pieces of rice straw drifted through the air; a huge billow of smoke rose and was driven toward the building. Finally all the new pine panels were in splinters. The smoke and fire went on as men passed out the splinters to eagerly reaching hands in the crowd.

Moromi Cranes

In the shrines on *Nagasaki* hill
Where the bomb kept time with eternity
Festoons of colorful *origami* cranes
Turn *Nagasaki* into a prayer.

On the other side of *Kyushu* in *Fukuoka*
The *Moromi* River widens at the mouth through rocked up banks
As it reaches through the artificial beaches of *Momochihama*
On half-filled or half-empty *Hakata* Bay.

It was in *Hakata* Bay that the typhoon swamped
The Mongol Armada and saved Japan
From the fate of death in 1187
With a *Kamikaze* Divine Wind.

In the *Moromi* River bottom when the tide is out
Moromi Cranes stalk the mudflats one foot at a time,
In dirty white feathers and Hip-hop crest,
With spike legs and intently focused eyes.

The *Moromi* Cranes acquired more company when the tide went
    way out.
Clammers, oyster gatherers, children and mothers in rubber boots,
Fishermen who ordinarily poled from the fraying edges,
Went down in extraordinary numbers to comb the mud for food.

Midway across the *Moromi* suspended in space and capped with
    a crane
The median thrust of a new highway bridge hung in the incomplete
    monumental air
For months until spring came and construction recommenced the
    ratcheting out
Of section by section as the bridge unfolded through space towards
The hill in *Atagohama* with a *Shinto* Shrine on its indelicate top.

I see cranes by the intricate triangle lattice work dozens
Topping off half-baked buildings, constructing and deconstructing
      real estate
From platforms of civic permission
While the white birds screech and take a darting step
When there was nothing worth sticking a neck out and a beak in
      the mud for.
The tide raised the boats and set them back down in the mud.

I wanted another language bright enough to write in,
Found instead a towering monument of superficially deferential
      social control,
Found my escape hatch shattered in a broken talky dream,
Sought gustatory salvation in *yaki soba* and *nambam tori* or
      barbarian chicken.

I'll probably never get back to *Nagasaki*
Or anywhere else in intensified Japan,
Where I dug not the answer I was looking for
Out from under three or more distinct kinds of exfoliating cranes,
Out of the matrix in *Fukuoka*,
Out of my mind and ordinary life for awhile,
Before lifting my tired mistaken eyes to watch
What was going on around me
Turn staler by degrees in the trapped sunset.

The Middle Kingdom

The *Xiang Jiang* River Bridge

The *Xiang* River Bridge over Orange Island
Swarms in both directions in the morning connecting
The east and west halves of *Changsha* back together.

On the jut at the south end where the island parts
The rapid muddy water flowing north,
I defied the sleeping authorities in the dark,
By climbing over the fence to go down to the edge
Before dawn in the as yet unopened park,
To pay homage to Mao Zedong.

Listen to the waves lap and ripple,
The sound of barges going by both ways.
Zhongguo, Hunan, Changsha, Juzhou.

Rooted in space the mystery intensifies
Languages traveling in opposite directions.
Orange Island, Long Beach, South Lake, China.

Zheng He

In 1414 *Zheng He*, a *Ming* dynasty admiral,
pushed his fleet to the eastern edge of Africa.

In 1492 Columbus had three ships of one deck
apiece which together weighed 415 tons
accompanied by one hundred other men.

Zheng He had sixty-two galleons and more than a
hundred auxiliary vessels. The largest galleons had
three decks on the poop alone, and each of them
weighed about 1,500 tons. They had nine masts and
twelve sails, and are said to have measured 440 feet
long by 180 feet wide. In *Zheng He's* fleet were:

868 civil officers, 26,800 soldiers, 93 commanders,
two senior commanders, 140 "millerions" [captains
of a thousand men, (battalion level commanders)],
403 centurions, a Senior Secretary of the Board of
Revenue, a geomancer, a military instructor, two
military judges, 180 medical officers and assistants,
two orderlies, seven senior eunuch ambassadors, ten
junior eunuchs and 53 eunuch chamberlains, along
with an unspecified number of signalers, interpreters,
scribes, professional negotiators, purveyors, Chinese
and foreign navigators, helmsmen, military and civil
mechanics, naval captains, common sailors and cooks.

Philip Snow,
The Star Raft: China's Encounter with Africa,
p 21-22, 1988

Finding the Middle of the Middle Kingdom

In the landlocked approximate geographical center of China
In the red earthed province of *Hunan*
Near the village of *Shaoshan* hanging in the rafters
Of Mao Zedong's boyhood farm home
Hangs a moldboard plow his family used
To turn the soil in the cradle of the Mao Dynasty.

Hunan is and means "south of the lake,"
South of the Yangtze, the *Chang Jiang* river,
With a capitol city of *Changsha*
Where Mao went to college.
Liu Shao Ch'i and *Lin Piao*
Also called *Hunan* home
Where the revolution began.

Mao recognized a serious problem and took it seriously.
The imperative was to rid China of foreign domination.
The impulse was sound; the effort was successful.
The Peoples Republic of China was proclaimed
At *Tian An Men* on the first of October, 1949.

They only had to overcome by turns
The ignorance of the indifferent, disorganized and exploited peasants;
The Quisling, criminal ineptitude of the *Kuo Min Tang*;
The rapacious, murderous, invading Japanese,
And the bellicose, blustering, ignorant Americans under Truman.

The people beat in other words
The hitherto three best organized fascist systems in their way.

The southern American ignoramuses ignored their own
Native born, native speaking, natural understanding people
In the State Department in the Chinese diplomatic field in favor of
A right-wing whacko military solution.

China is necklaced in by offshore islands
Not always under the control of friendly fire.

China is a Pacific power by insinuation
And being 49 years into the full swing
Of the expansive pulsation phase of the Maoist dynasty
Truly has time as well as space on its side.

Chinmen (*Quemoy*) and *Matsu Dao*
Right off the coast but controlled from Taiwan
Were shelled in a test of the American electorate in 1960.

The *Ryukyu* Islands which stand above the sea
In a gossamer semi-circle from *Kagoshima* on *Kyushu* to Taipei
Have formerly been under Chinese suzerainty.
Okinawa and the *Ryukyus* are now administered from Tokyo
As an American military base.
There can be an *Okinawa* independent of Tokyo and D.C.
But not an *Okinawa* independent of other people's military power.
Meet the terror of the expendable pawns and stones
In the search for the global *Go* solutions.

Hainan Dao off the south coast in the South China Sea
Almost in the Gulf of Tonkin near North Vietnam
Is three-fourths the size of Taiwan.

Across *Dagat* are the 10,000 islands of the Philippines.
Further south are the myriad islands of Indonesia and Australia.
Through the *Formosa* Straits,
(I like that Portuguese word, *Formosa*.
It means "beautiful isle.")
Blow the tropical summer winds toward Japan.

The competition for economic expansion is chiefly with
The Americans and their Japanese surrogates.
China has a border beef with every country they share an edge with.
They know how to run a bluff
Like lobbing rockets into the water around Taipei
During the very belated, quasi-democratic election of *Lee Tung Hui.*

For public relations purposes
The more Taiwan can resemble a democracy
The easier it will be for the United States to defend it.
That wasn't the case when *Chaing Kai Shek* and the *Kuo Min Tang*
Superimposed their two million refugees
Onto several layers of more native Taiwanese.

In those days anybody who wasn't communist
No matter how brutal the dictatorship
Could be supported by the American military
Taking their cues from J. Edgar Hoover of the FBI.

Now that there are no longer any communists in this picture
The basis for military control of the regional economy
Will gradually shift to the Chinese until
They can remind the Japanese of how close together they really are.
The heart of *Sun Tzu* commands respect
For *The Art of War* and a patient
Biding of time until
The propitious moment arrives to be seized.

In the middle of The Middle Kingdom
In over a billion beating hearts
Rises the wellspring of eternal Chinese hope
For a decent meal, a little space,
And among the youngsters learning English
The chance to get out of China.

As more and more people get out of China
Under the impetus of the English intervention
Which started 200 years ago
And went through some horrific Opium Wars,
Boxer Rebellions,
The century long British open market in Hong Kong,
And the Americans picking up what slack they could
When the British folded the Union Jack,
More and more people will want to

150

Get out of China
To Vancouver, Toronto, New York and Brisbane.

Nobody ever stops being Chinese
Even when they have American passports.

Time won't tell you
What linguistic geography can:
The Chinese and the English pile up the objects of their affection
At the end of sentences when they are well made.
The Chinese move as a *Danwei* or unit.
The speakers of English accumulate cash
For retired shareholders still acting out
The dysfunctional behaviors of
Thornstein Veblen's *Theory of the Leisure Class.*

In the days of *Zheng He* when the Indian Ocean
Could have become a Chinese Lake if they'd chosen
600 years ago not to abandon
Mombasa, Mogadishu, the Straits of *Hormuz*
For the Grand Canal from Nanjing to Beijing
And an interior waterway succumbing to
"The high level equilibrium trap" and retreating
To the Straits of *Malacca* where one of the great
Chinese cities still stands.

Singapore, we've neglected you
But we're on our way back.

Chairman Mao Returns to *Shaoshan*

Chairman Mao goes back
To his hometown
After 32 years
In the blinding grip of power.

What can farm lads see in the soil
After all this time,
The red soil of *Hunan*
Nurturing rice and revolution.

"Bitter sacrifice strengthens bold resolve"
Recalling his dim dreams and cursing the past
The hero of nutrition floats in on
"Wave upon wave of paddy and beans."

I was a teenage farm lad in Idaho
Ignorant of the ways of the world.

It's been ten big years
Since I taxied to *Shaoshan*
An ugly American
With Asian friends.

We blew through a funeral
Procession in the village
Firecrackers, gongs,
And dust thrown up by revolving tires.

"*Cao Nide Xing,*"
The cyclist cursed
Through the window
At the cabbie

Who nearly knocked him off
The edge of the road
Into a rice paddy.
It means: Fuck your face.

In the Garden of Mao

In the yard in front of Mao Zedong's
Boyhood home,

Three young Chinese men,
Slightly drunk,
Make friends with me.

Their exuberance overcomes
My miserable Mandarin.

One of them insists
On holding hands with me.

His is hot, drunk.
It's April and we're only
500 *kilometres* north of *Guangzhou.*

The Case of the Shrinking Mandarin

You can never go back to where you've been.
Both you and it will have changed
No matter how short the mean time.

How much you change is a record of pressure
Applied or deflected to the basic neutrinos.

Better to stay put in the body that brought you.
It's changing fast enough but would your hand
Hold the keys to the language revolution
If only a tongue can be put to it?

Rereading my *Changsha* file I fall
In love with my big trip far from home.

Staring at maps which are conceptual territory
Shrunk by distortion to the larger parts of
A two dimensional redundancy.

The map of language making is an echo of choices
Made in the past and passed forward to now
Which disappears the moment I acknowledge it.

From *pictogram* to *ideogram*
Through *logogram* to *phonogram*,
The grams have it which should be graphs.

Such mitochondrion *morphografs*
As get transmitted in the post synaptic thickening
Make it difficult for a *Zhongguo Ren* to separate himself
From what he has just said.

No esthetic distance is too great to fall for in English.
The ambiguity impediment is resolved in context,
Supposing you can stay in context
And not mindread your listeners into a
Close at hand form of your other selves.

Keep the *Haizimen* in context for if
They learn by rote they would have difficulty
Transferring to context.

Kalgren claims there were 3700 syllables in *T'ang*.
Now in Mao they're down to 1300.

Why are the syllables reduced by a factor of three to one
Where the mapping ratio has become one to ten
Characters per sound
While the true ratio is one to sixty
And the ambiguity grows over time?

Since the purpose of language is disambiguation
How and why did Mandarin acquire its apparent *metapurpose*
Of disambiguating close at hand to accelerate ambiguity at greater
        remove?

How many hidden benefits can be ascribed to
Accelerating ambiguity?
Stay in the context, stay in the conversation
Stay close or the conspiracy abandons you
And you get suspicious that
You don't know what people are talking about
And you're right.

Keeping power a secret is the secret to its successful application.
This top down approach to governmental oppression
Finds its reflections at the hearth.

Victimized by their own suspicion people project:
If I'm doing it everybody else must be too.
So who would you trust to tell the truth.

The phonological recombination of juxtaposed morphemes
Broadens the vocabulary and the trust.

When *Fa Yu* is French and *Yu Fa* is grammar
And both *Fa* and *Yu* are the same characters
The popbead flexibility of vocabulary building
A syllabary stake through the ears of time
Parabolizes toward the infinite.

So what language is this that I speak when I want to
Run back down the length of Orange Island
Honing my chops in my head as I jog and sweat in
        the pre-dawn beauty
Saying "Hello" to every *Haizimen* on foot and bicycle
On their way to school and the rest of their lives
As morning brightens everything in *Hunan* up.

Testing Our Metal

The tungsten mine at Patterson in
Pahsimeroi closed down
The very day the armistice at
Panmunjom was signed.

The Slowboat to China

Never mind this animal has been in the water
Already around 200 years and may take
Another 100 to reach the coves of Cathay.

On the other hand it could get there in 20
Upsetting a few right wing apple carts
As bad as the expulsion of *Chaing Kai Shek* to Taiwan once did.

Formosa the beautiful isle in *Portugalese*
Across the *Formosa* Strait through which
The tropical wind toward Japan has barely ever ceased to blow
A Chinese whisper in their general direction.

Out here on the edge beyond China proper the improper
Beijing bandits have a border beef
With everyone they have a border with.

Vietnam, India, Russia, the islands of
The South China Sea, *Dagat,* to say nothing of
Their preoccupation of *Xizang* or Tibet and *Yunnan.*

If this doesn't mean anything to Kansas in the middle
Of the middling kingdom where English is misspoken
You could *Osawatomie* right out of my sun baked soul.

I Want to Get Out of China

The British aristocrat Philip Larkin once quipped
"I wouldn't mind visiting China
If I could come back the same day."

Such is the depth self-inflicted sarcasm has sunk to
Allow us to see ourselves in English in
Reversing if/would to negative wouldn't/if.

English is a Chinese language now,
Chinese as a possessive adjective
Not a nominal glomming onto whatever works.

I never met a young Chinese who could speak English
Who didn't divulge the entitle-ing phrase to me,
"I want to get out of China."

Considering how crowded most parts of China are
The desire is understandable.
Where are they going to go?

To rot in ships off of Vancouver Island?
In containers through Panama to New York?
Australia and Canada are thinly populated promised lands.

The dragon stirs
Fries its mind
With potential.

Mu &
The Magic Character Reader Sorter Optical Scanner
for Dr. Litke

Why should the word "trees,"
No better or worsely printed
Than all the rest of the words in the text of
"Uproar & Feedback"
Come through the Hewlett Packard Scanjet 4S as
"*Mu*,"
The word for trees in
Sumerian and Chinese?

When they cut the *mu* along the Portneuf?

If Would

If Would is a basic Indo-European premise
Otherwise how would we have gotten so far
Out of the caves since the last deglaciation
If we hadn't have been exercising
The most appealing choice of many options?

If Would is missing in Mandarin
According to the sage of Swarthmore, Alfred Bloom.
Taking up the tongs of his comprehension
I haven't been able to locate it either.

To give you an example *Pei Min Xin* in 1990,
A spokesman for the nascent democracy in China movement
After the Massacre at *Tian An Men* square
By The Butcher of Beijing, *Deng Xiaoping,*
Spoke in Walla Walla of the aspirations of would be
        Chinese democrats.

Pei Min Xin at the time was a student at Harvard Law
And gave such a good speech in English
He caught himself making a half dozen
Performance errors in English
And corrected them as he went along
Much as a native speaker of English would.

After the speech in our fashion
Pei fielded questions from the capacity crowd in Village Hall
On the campus at Walla Walla College
With alacrity and aplomb befitting a man comfortable
With his role as a popularizer in front of a sympathetic audience.

However when Tim Wolf,
A young reporter from the *Union Bulletin,*
Asked him the following question
He wavered back and forth shifting his weight
From one foot to another for forty-five seconds:

Do you think given all that's happened in the past year
In eastern Europe with the collapse of communism in
East Germany, Hungary, Poland and Czechoslovakia,
That *if* the student demonstrations in *Tian An Men*
Had taken place this spring instead of last
That the outcome *would* have been different?"

Here was about as big an If Would question
As any Chinese wannabe democrat could get asked
And *Pei Min Xin* said, after forty-five seconds:
"I can't answer that question."

"What I can tell you is that since
Gorbachev and the Russian communist party were able
To see all the scorn and opprobrium heaped on *Deng Xiaoping*
And the Chinese for overreacting,
It may have made it easier for them to let go of Eastern Europe."

What seemed to me to have taken place
In this nonscientific, anecdotal, poetic instance was
The If Would overwhelmed *Pei Min Xin's* considerable
         capacities in English
By dropping him back into Mandarin where
He felt obligated to put the events
Back into concrete consequential order,
S*ince*, then may have.

Maybe something else entirely happened.
Mind reading is not as effective as mind saying
And nothing can replace mind doing something
With materials at hand,
Just don't call it "thinking" in my presence.

I've yet to meet a native speaker of Mandarin
Who can answer these kinds of questions in English which require
Random concrete if not abstract random configurations
In order to make sense out of things.

"In German *oder* English, I can count down,
And I'm learning Chinese said Werner Von Braun."
So sang Tom Lear and in German and English
An infinite series of If Woulds allowed or enabled
Europeans to take most of the world over and Europeanize it by
selective choices.

2

If it was an If Would choice negatively made
By the masters of *Zheng He's* Star Raft fleet in
The Indian Ocean in the 1400s
That stimulated the contraction back to Beijing
On inland waterways and a retreat
To the Straits of *Malacca*
That Africa and the world were not worth having,
Would it make any difference?

You can't get very far out of the conversation in Mandarin
Before you're completely lost.
English speakers on the other hand,
"Dr. Livingstone, I presume?"
Pride themselves on getting lost by themselves
Where not even their mothers can find them.

If China continues to expand this time
In concentric circles from the middle of the Middle Kingdom
Having at the moment a border dispute
With everyone they share a border with
How much of it would we be able to attribute to
Their exposure to the South Sea Barbarians in English via
The Opium Wars, the Boxer Rebellions,
The short end of the return to Hong Kong stick?

History takes place in the structure of language operating on
Geography
Distributed in asymmetrical time.

If I were to get to go
Out to lunch or dinner again
With *Hi Yamadasan* back to the *Huodong Fangdian*
Fire Palace restaurant,
Mao Zedong's favorite,
On *Pozi Jie* street [my own name!] in the heart of *Changsha*
Would we be any better off walking back up
Another two-bicycle-wide narrow street and bumping into
A birthday celebration for *Liu Shao Ch'i*
With a disgruntled reveler holding on to the pail of
A tin bucket full of firecrackers going off
In their limited directions
Than we were in the first place?

Chinese If Would Tripping to Mars
(A very red planet)

If the ocean was a flower
And I was a bee
I'd suck it dry
And we'd already be there.

Beijing Time

Between four and four-thirty AM I watch the light reappear
In my part of the world,
Reading ten year old notes from Beijing
Suggesting the aspect particle "*le*" indicates
Something happened in another space
Rather than before in time.

We stack space
We tell time
Where to get off.

Time and space
Do we have any or enough of either?
It could be something else entirely
That we find ourselves in.

Pacific Century Runs Aground

(3 years before it got started, January, 1998)

With all that happy talk
The Asian tigers tied their tails together
And went down swinging.

San ge laohu, san ge laohu, paode kwai, paode kwai
Ige meiyo weiba, ige meiyo weiba, zen chi quai, zen chi quai.

The folk tales of the devouring
Interests rates still set
In the twilight towns of London and New York.

The Pacific is wide and interest is high.
Steal and lend, steal and lend,
That will get you by.

PNTR
(Permanent Normal Trading Relations)

There's nothing normal about driving another
25-50 million more Chinese peasants, ie people,
Off the land and into the cities
However permanent it will turn out to be
Essential to global trading relations.

Certainly as normal as driving English peasants off the land
        to create London
Out of woolen mills from sheep's pasture
In those many metallic days at the commencement of
The Industrial Revolution began by the Enclosure Movement
And financed with the proceeds of the Slave Trade
When the rich traded their own people slums for land so that
"Sheep may safely graze."

The whipsawed white American peasants
Homesteaded out onto the land in Lincoln-Marxist fashion
Then dust bowled back and agribusinessed off of it
A few living generations later
Had their innings in this international pastime.

There is blood in peasant eyes
Tears in their armpits.
No sweat quacks the lame duck president
To the last Republican on earth.

PNTR

(take two, they're small)

The day PNTR passed
Was the last day of the first part of our lives.

Permanent Normal Trading Relations
Has a hollow English nominalistic ring.

Permanent itself a single word oxymoron
Laughing in the face of the people who spit it out.

Nothing is permanent let alone normal.
Doesn't mean mutually beneficial.

Trading Relations
Giving up some cousins for a few nephews?
We'll trade our peasants for a few more of yours.

Trading places as PNTR gives the kiss of permanence
To the transfer of industrial capacity Chinese ward.
Bu Zhi Dao, Bu Dong.

Remember the Cottonwoods

Cottonwoods bloom along Beijing avenues.
Seeds proliferate into the breeze and swirl into cotton drifts.
Wild yellow roses bloom in the courtyard of the Beijing hotel,
Identical to one that used to bloom
Below our kitchen window in Walla Walla
Until the Bur Oak tree or the blight killed it.

Cottonwoods thrive along the Little White and Two Strike
Rivers of South Dakota that flow
Through Crow Dog's Paradise
Known to Lakota as *waga chun.*

Cottonwoods were the trees I climbed in my Idaho youth
For the view, for the rush near the top,
My crotch in theirs
To risk hanging on to foot and claw
Clinging with my legs until I "came."

On the highway to Taos
Winding through a Rio Grande river bottom glen
I asked Norbert the driver how to say Cottonwood in Spanish.
"Alamo," he said, like "The Alamo."
Remember The Alamo! Remember the cottonwood.
Alamo must be Arabic: El-Al-Amo.
The the amo. Remember the ammo.
Te amo. Remember the love.

Cottonwood is soft wood
Vulnerable to human abuse.

Here in Taos were not that far from Los Alamos
Where nuclear secrets leak
Into Chinese like a verb of infinite absorption and dispersal.

The big secret is the Al-phabet
Also Arabic and already out.

Remember the Alamo
Remember the cottonwood
Remember the *waga chun*
Take time to pray for the trees.

The Vegetable Market

The plow in the rafters of Chairman Mao's house
Is the moldboard key to the free vegetable market.

First to plow and first to plant
Vegetables in rows,
Half the things we take for granted
Have a Chinese point of origination.

The Chinese led the world in startling developments
Including a huge and well fed population,
Until the so-called Industrial Revolution.

Today as one by-product of all those vegetables,
There are too many people trapped in too little time,
Not enough space, and a controlled imagination.

China sleeps like a dragon
The rest of the world curiously circles.

Barefoot *Hunan* Rice Paddy Boy

"What the hell would I know,
I'm just a barefoot *Hunan*
Rice paddy boy," John's father claims,
Invoking his peasant background.

He was in the *Kuo Min Tang* air force,
Shot down over Burma,
He wound up recuperating in France
As the *Kuo Min Tang's* liaison with
Gaullest France.

He gives everybody shit.
The Government, the PLA,
The students,
The goddess of democracy
Doesn't cut any ice with him,
A plaster of Paris original.

The Redwall Cafe

From the joint venture seats in the Redwall Cafe,
It's easy to see the ordinary flow of China pass by.

I jogged *Tian An Men Gong Chang* in my *Cuneiform* bra,
Would have made a great ad in the middle fifties.

It was a great mistake to visit the Great Wall
At *Ba Da Ling* on May Day.

There are so many people here about as
Free as flies in amber.

From rice paddy overload to charcoal tofu,
I'll savor those meals for a lifetime.

Charcoal Tofu

At the Fire Palace Restaurant
On *Pozi Jie* street,
The platters of charcoal tofu
Resemble square briquets.
They live up to their real name:
Chou Dou Fu or malodorous bean curd.

Even the Chinese scholars don't eat them,
Electing to nibble as their bald heads break
Out with beads of sweat
From the spicier dishes,
Like kelp in pepper sauce.

I'd go back to the *Huo Gong Dian* once a week
If I lived anywhere near *Changsha,*
To savor the dishes I never had time to
And remind myself of the ones I love.

The Azaleas of *Changsha*

for *Sheng Zhi*

Who has not looked gratefully at flowers
And thought, you're very recent, at first bloom.
Realize the roots of this and every flower,
Even from the lobby of the Lotus Hotel,
Reach back to the first sea.

Some people think Americans,
Have shallow history,
Easily learnable and dismissed,
Not remembering or taking into account,
The continents, deserts, and mountains,
Oceans and seas our variegated people crossed,
Babbling in a multitude of tongues,
Entire languages and libraries, Bibles on our backs,
Accumulating Celticity and exterminating natives,
Even only in human form.

In April the Azaleas are blooming on the streets,
In the parks, up *Yue Lu Shan* mountain, and
Back in the lobbies of the *Lu Rong* hotel where
The International Conference on the Computerization of Chinese
And other Oriental languages is in full swing.

Here the flowers of the face of man are shining, in
Azaleas, the *Shi Huar* or city flower of Changsha,
With reflected light through widened irises,
The wide opened eyes of men and women wanting
To believe and understand there is not
A mean one among them.

Beijing with Cottonwoods and Roses

for Bei Dao

On Earth Day in Beijing,
I'll be on the prowl around,
Tian An Men Gong Chang,
Sifting the displaced Gobi Desert sand,
For clues to the rectangularicity,
Of the Middle Kingdom's cyto architecture.

Few places on earth exhibit any more past,
Than the squares and layers of Beijing,
Where I stalk the corridors of palatial additions,
To the Beijing *Fang Dian* hand in hand with
Direct descendants of Beijing Man.

Unearthing answers to my twenty question quiz on
The suitability of Mandarin for the modern world,
I come across a grammatical rule via Alfred Bloom,
That if it has no signifier for counter factuals,
How would an alternative future ever be imagined?

J. Paul Getty, the business suitable curmudgeon,
Made a fortune investing in contrary markets,
Where everybody's selling and nobody's buying.
"Hold your coins 'til there's blood in the streets."
China is a buyer's market.

They've cleaned the blood up around here very nicely,
From the Beijing Massacre of 1989,
But they haven't cleaned the hairsplitting language up,
Of the most favorable take, most favored nation,
On why and where the actual killing took place on
Dong or *Xi Chang An Jie* avenue paralleling the square.

Where does the square end and the street begin,
That could unlock the truth of the Forbidden City,
And wash out the lies of interlocking squares,
Held together with suspicion and palmed rigidly
Off on the world as inscrutable mystery?

The utter middle of the Middle Kingdom,
Has no center and its law can't be located with
Hermaphroditic calipers in hyper space,
Surrounded as it is by twelve million people
With low blood sugar assuming the posture
Of a nationwide passive aggressive slump.

Bangzhu Haizimen—Bangzhu Dajia—Shijie Xiandiahua
Can sound like a call for a speedy trial,
The West lost the capacity to deliver the right to
21 days between arrest and a bullet in the back
Of the head, and literally means:
Help the children—Help everybody—Modernize the world.

The joint venture partner in the Palace Hotel,
The *Jie Fang Jun*, aka the People's Liberation Army,
Yanked the charter out from under the Beijing
Museum of Modern Art for architectural extravagance.

Wake the town and shoot the people
Won't win any prizes for originality in government.
The desperate acts of desperate men, desperately
Driving the people deeper into the convulsive past,
Define the cave in to geriatric Fascism.

"What does retirement mean in China?" a banner in
Hanzi on *Tian An Men* before the massacre asked.
"It's when 80 year old men
Order meetings with 70 year old men
To force the retirement of 60 year old men."

Trapped on the fringe in authoritarian language,
Bei Da, Guangzhou, Hong Kong, and Tibet,
The tangled hearts of the people will yield,
To the irresistible urge to speak without fear.
Why colonize your own people?

The trouble with the Middle Kingdom on edge is,
The farther you go from the center of empire,
The weaker the circuits of power.

English is the language of freedom.
Free speech is the flywheel of the English advance,
From the plains of Kent to the public television
Classless rooms of a Beijing kindergarten,
Ying Yu the language and the character for
Brave to be so far from home.

The chances for democracy in China,
Are neither good nor fat nor slim.
The Gate of Heavenly Peace was open until you closed it.
On a spherical earth, the circle cannot be squared.

The Tao of Physics

The dusty Mercedes
Full of secret police
Watch the embassy for
Fang Li Zhi.

Fast Forward
(May, 1990)

On the United flight back to Seattle from Hong Kong,
The day I got back before I started,
Flying asymmetrically into the clenched teeth of time,
Amusing myself in *Mona Lisa Overdrive*,
Feeling bad about the 20th Century,
I saved enough time to defy it.

As far as I'm concerned, it's history,
Though I'm surrounded by people,
Still gearing up for the nineties.

There was a decade that was over before it began.

Be done with it and don't let it try to surprise you,
With cataclysmic upheavals, mass arrests,
Or a climactic debauching at the millennial terminus.

Flight From Hong Kong

Are the speakers of English really preparing a retreat
So that greater China can reassemble itself
On the ruins of its irreputable past?

Ming Dynasty Confucian dingbats suspended
Like flies in the marketplace of anger in,
"The high level equilibrium trap,"
Where the plans for *Zheng He's* boats were burned,
Who beat the American Salvation Army to Mogadishu
By six hundred years, have no one to blame but themselves.

China discovered Africa was of no particular consequence
To the centripetal force that forced the hand that held the shovel
That dug the ditch that
Turned into the Grand Canal.

The English discovered their civilization in Africa
Where they sufficiently impressed enough slave labor
To carry themselves over the industrial threshold.

China has always had labor to burn and turned
Their back on Africa where the marriage of capitalism and
Slavery was left to the speakers of English to consummate.

Certain speakers of English are beginning to go hungry
In search for new places to plunder on their
Cinderella burnout, smothered with arms and
Relying on force to "finesse" their problems.

The empty tin cup of Texas rattling around the Middle East
Is bringing not the end of history, as one enlightened
Japanese historian imagined it, but rather more of the same.

Remember your history, practice your salute, polish your brass,
Shoot somebody, blow something up, fumble forward.
If there's a draft in here, dodge it.

Mao rid China of foreign domination.
Does Hong Kong belong to China, itself, or the world?

The speakers of English rid most of North America of opposition to
      their empire,
Which doesn't travel well and is
Fated to squander its resources wishing that it would.

The small birds in the wisteria next door,
Like peasants everywhere who can,
Will wisely stay out of the way.

I Wanted to End With a Crescendo

I wanted to end with a crescendo.
What I got was a sprawl.
That's what language does to you.
You wind up in little groups talking to yourselves in
Mama Loshen, the mother tongue.
Using slang you won't have to worry about
Being misunderstood in.

If you are being addressed from the Great Hall of the People
Rest assured that you are being lied to and mislead
In *Patrispeckt*, the language of the father land.

The mother and father language conflict.
Permeates, pervades, and penetrates.

Poetry is written in *Mama Loshen*
Orders are given in *Patrispeckt*.
Which language do you dare speak when?

The White Crane Springs
for Robert McNealy

Robert gave me
A smooth brown stone
The size of a Canadian quarter
To leave in China
In exchange for one
He took years ago from *Si Chuan.*

I complete the geologic
Transfer to
A niche above the
White Crane Springs.

Intellectual Background

Intellectual Background for *Across the North Pacific*

This selected bibliography is intended to demonstrate the range of materials examined. It does not include a large number of more generally applicable works in English on the history, politics, language, geography and economics of the North Pacific Region.

Bloom, Alfred, *The Linguistic Shaping of Thought: A Study in the Impact of Language on Thinking in China and the West*, Lawrence Erlbaum Associates, Hillsdale, NJ:1981

Beidelman, T.O., Editor, *The Translation of Culture*, Tavistock, London:1971

Benedict, Ruth, *The Chrysanthemum and the Sword*, Meridian, The New American Library, New York:1974

Brannen, Christalyn and Wilen, Tracey, *Doing Business with Japanese Men: A Woman's Handbook*, Stone Bridge Press, Berkeley:1993

Choy, Rita Mei-Wah, *Understanding Chinese: A Guide to the Usage of Chinese Characters*, China West Books, San Francisco:1989

Christopher, Robert C., *The Japanese Mind: The Goliath Explained*, Tuttle, Tokyo:1983

Computer Processing of Oriental Languages, An International Journal of the Oriental Languages Computer Society, Department of Computer Science, National Tsing Hua University, Taiwan, ROC:1987-Present, thirteen quarterly volumes.

De Mente, Boye Lafayette, *Behind the Japanese Bow: An In-depth Guide to Understanding and Predicting Japanese Behavior*, Passport Books, a division of NTC, Lincolnwood, IL:1993
Chinese Etiquette & Ethics in Business, NTC Business Books, Lincolnwood, IL:1989

Doi, Takeo, M.D., *Amae No Kozo, (The Anatomy of Dependence)*, translated by John Bester, Kodansha, Tokyo:1981
Omote To Ura (The Anatomy of Self: The Individual Versus Society), translated by Mark A. Harbison, Kodansha, Tokyo:1985

Farmer, Kathleen Ann, *Modularity in Syntax: A Study of Japanese and English*, MIT, Cambridge:1984

Fischer, David Hackett, *The Great Wave: Price Revolutions and the Rhythm of History*, Oxford, New York:1996

Friedman, George, & Lebard, Meredith, *The Coming War with Japan*,
St. Martin's Press, New York:1991

Fukutake, Tadashi, *The Japanese Social Structure: Its Evolution in the
Modern Century*, 2nd edition, translated with a forward by
Ronald P. Dore, University of Tokyo, Tokyo:1989

Gibney, Frank, *Japan: The Fragile Superpower*, 2nd revised edition,
Charles Tuttle, Vermont, Tokyo:1985

Gluck, Carol, *Japan's Modern Myths: Ideology in the Late Meiji
Period*, Princeton, Princeton, NJ:1985

Hansen, Chad, "Classical Chinese Philosophy as Linguistic Analysis,"
Journal of Chinese Philosophy #14, Dialogue Publishing
Company, Honolulu:1987

Jansen, Maurius B., *The Making of Modern Japan*, Belknap/Harvard,
Cambridge/London:2000

Jaynes, Julian, *The Origin of Consciousness in the Breakdown of the
Bicameral Mind*, Houghton Mifflin, Boston:1976

Kaplan, David E., and Dubro, Alec, *Yakuza: The Explosive Account of
Japan's Criminal Underworld*, Macmillan, New York:1986

Kapp, Robert A., Editor, *Communicating with China* (For the China
Council of the Asia Society, Inc.), Intercultural Press, Inc.,
Chicago:1983

Kasper, Gabriele, Editor, *Pragmatics of Japanese as Native and Target
Language*, University of Hawaii, Manoa:1992

Korzybski, Alfred, *Science and Sanity: An Introduction to Non-
Aristotelian Systems and General Semantics*, The Institute of
General Semantics, Lakeville, CT:1958

Kuno, Susumu, *The Structure of the Japanese Language*, MIT,
Cambridge:1973

Lebra, Takie Sugiyama, Editor, *Japanese Patterns of Behavior*,
University of Hawaii, Honolulu:1976

Levy, Marion J. Jr., *The Family Revolution in Modern China*,
Atheneum, New York:1968

Lewis, Richard, D., *When Cultures Collide: Managing Successfully
Across Cultures*, Nicholas Brealey Publishing, London:1996

Li, Charles N., and Thomspon, Sandra A., *Mandarin Chinese: A
Functional Reference Grammar*, University of California Press,
Berkeley:1989

Lin, Helen T., *Essential Grammar for Modern Chinese*, Cheng & Tsui
Company, Boston:1981

Logan, Robert K., *The Alphabet Effect: The Impact of the Phonetic*

Alphabet on the Development of Western Civilization, William Morrow and Co., Inc. New York:1986

Macleod, Robert, *China Inc.: How to Do Business with the Chinese,* Bantam, Toronto:1988

Mao Zedong, *Guerrilla Warfare,* translated with an introduction by Brigadier General Samuel B. Griffith, USMC (ret.), Praeger, New York:1961

Merton, Thomas, *The Way of Chuang Tzu,* New Directions, New York:1969

Miyamoto, Masao, M.D., *Straitjacket Society: An Insider's Irreverent View of Bureaucratic Japan,* translated by Juliet Winters Carpenter, Kodansha, Tokyo:1994

Miller, Roy Andrew, *Japan's Modern Myth: The Language and Beyond,* Weatherhill, New York & Tokyo:1982

Murphy, R. Taggart, *The Real Price of Japanese Money,* Weidenfeld & Nicolson, London:1996

Najita, Tetsuo, and Scheiner, Irwin, *Japanese Thought in the Tokugawa Period, 1600-1868; Methods and Metaphors,* Chicago University Press, Chicago:1978

Nakamura, Hajime, *Ways of Thinking of Eastern Peoples,* University of Hawaii Press, Honolulu: 1971

Nakane, Chie, *Japanese Society,* Penguin, Middlesex, England:1973

Nathan, John, *Sony: The Private Life,* Houghton Mifflin, New York: 1999

Niyekawa, Agnes M., *Minimum Essential Politeness: A Guide to the Japanese Honorific Language,* Kodansha, Tokyo:1991

Norman, Jerry, *Chinese,* Cambridge Language Surveys Series, Cambridge, London:1988

Ohmae, Kenichi, *The End of the Nation State: The Rise of Regional Economies,* HarperCollins, London:1995

Ozawa, Ichiro, *Blueprint for a New Japan: The Rethinking of a Nation,* translated by Louisa Rubinfien, Kodansha, Tokyo:1995

Ozawa, Terutomo, *Japan's Technological Challenge to the West, 1950-1974: Motivation and Accomplishment,* MIT, Cambridge:1974

Pascale, Richard Tanner, and Athos, Anthony G., *The Art of Japanese Management: Applications for American Executives,* Warner Books, Inc. New York:1981

Pinker, Steven, *How the Mind Works,* Norton, New York:1997
The Language Instinct: How the Mind Creates Language,

William Morrow and Co., Inc. New York:1994

Pye, Lucian W., *Asian Power and Politics: The Cultural Dimensions of Authority*, Belknap/Harvard, Cambridge:1985

Ramsey, S. Robert, *The Languages of China*, Princeton University Press, Princeton, NJ:1987

Reischauer, Edwin O., *The Japanese*, Belknap/Harvard, Cambridge: 1978
My Life Between Japan and America, Weatherhill, Tokyo:1986

Reischauer, Haru Matsukata, *Samurai and Silk: A Japanese and American Heritage*, Tuttle, Tokyo:1986

Renfrew, Colin, *Archaeology & Language: The Puzzle of Indo-European Origins*, Cambridge, New York: 1987

Rong, Shen, *At Middle Age*, Panda Books, Beijing:1987

Sadler, A.L., *The Life of Shogun Tokugawa Ieyasu: The Maker of Modern Japan*, George Allen & Unwin Ltd. 1937, Tuttle, Tokyo:1987

Shibitani, Masayoshi, *The Languages of Japan*, Language Survey Series, Cambridge, London:1990

Snow, Edgar, *Red Star Over China*, Grove Press, New York:1968

Soros, George, *The Alchemy of Finance: Reading the Mind of the Market*, John Wiley & Sons, New York:1987

Sun Tzu, *The Art of War*, translated with an introduction by Samuel B. Griffith, Oxford University Press, London:1963

Suzuki, Takao, *Words in Context: A Japanese Perspective on Language and Culture*, translated by Akira Miura, Kodansha, Tokyo:1978

Tasker, Peter, *The Japanese: A Major Exploration of Modern Japan*, Truman Talley Books, E.P. Dutton, New York:1987, first published as *Inside Japan* by Siegwick and Jackson Limited in Great Britain.

Tien, H. Yuan, *China's Population Struggle: Demographic Decisions of the People's Republic, 1949-1969*, Ohio State University Press, Columbus:1973

Temple, Robert, *The Genius of China*, introduced by Joseph Needham, Simon & Schuster Inc., New York:1989

Toland, John, *Occupation*, Tom Doherty Associates, New York:1987
The Rising Sun: The Decline and Fall of the Japanese Empire, 1936-1945, two volumes, Random House, New York:1970

Toynbee, Arnold J., *A Study of History*, six volumes, Oxford University Press, London, New York, Toronto:1951

Tsunoda, Tadanaobu, *The Japanese Brain: Uniqueness and Universality*, translated by Yoshinori Oiwa, Taishukan, Tokyo:1985

Van Wolfgren, Karel, *The Enigma of Japanese Power: The First Full-Scale Examination of the Inner Workings of Japan's Political/Industrial System*, Random House, New York:1990 *Nihon no Chishikijin e (To the Japanese Intellectuals)*, Madosha, Tokyo:1995

Vogel, Ezra F., *Japan as No.1: Lessons for America*, Harvard, Cambridge:1979

Vygotsky, L. S., *Thought and Language*, translated by Eugenia Hanfmann and Gertrude Vakar, MIT, Cambridge, MA:1981

Wagar, W. Warren, *A Short History of the Future*, The University of Chicago Press, Chicago and London:1989

Wells, H.G., *The Shape of Things to Come*, New York, Macmillian: 1933

Wood, Christopher, *The Bubble Economy: The Japanese Economic Collapse*, Tuttle, Tokyo:1993

Yamada, Hisao, *Certain Problems Associated with the Design of Input Keyboards for Japanese Writing*, Department of Information Science, University of Tokyo, Tokyo:1982

Yamamura, Kozo, and Hatch, Walter, *Asia in Japan's Embrace: Building a Regional Production Alliance*, Cambridge, London:1996

Zhang Xinxin and Sang Ye, *Chinese Lives: An Oral History of Contemporary China*, Pantheon, New York:1987

Slough Press

For twenty-seven years Slough Press has been publishing contemporary literature by authors who experiment with form to communicate with a wide audience and influence the culture positively. Many Slough authors including Pat Littledog, Marion Wink and Ricardo Sánchez have published with New York commercial publishers and received greater distribution and wider fame. Slough Press has received grants from the Texas Arts Commission and won numerous awards. A partial backlist:

Asnes, Fred, *These Little Worlds,* 1984 Austin Book Award winner, $5.95

Cotolo, Frank, *Pony Player,* $11.95

Durham, Daniel, *Song to Tame the Storm,* 1990 Austin Book Award winner, $9.95

Fontenot, Ken, *All My Stars and Animals,* 1988 Austin Book Award Winner, $5.95

Gilman, Charlotte, and Taylor, Chuck, The Yellow Wallpaper, The Wallpaper Replies, $9.95

Griffin, Larry D., *Airspace,* West Texas poet on Olson's declaration of space, $4.00

Huffstickler, Albert, *Pieces of Brandon,* $3.00

Russell-Ides, *Getting Dangerously Close to Myself,* poetry by a playwright, $9.95

Jaffe, Maggie, *The Body Politic,* $3.00

LoBosco, Rocco, *Across the Distance of Knives,* $4.00

McCann, Janet, *Dialogue with the Dog Catcher,* $4.00

Pounds, Wayne, *Proletarian Life,* $5.00

Sánchez, Ricardo, *Bertrand,* $7.95
Sánchez, Ricardo, *Brown Bear Honey Madness,* rare, $15.00

Soloman, Sherry, *The Jumping Off Place,* 1989 Austin Book Award Winner, $6.95

St. Germain, Sheryl, *Making Bread at Midnight,* first edition, rare, $15.00
     second edition with author's postscript on craft, $9.95

Taylor, Chuck, *What Do You Want, Blood?,* 1988 Austin Book Award Winner, $5.95

To order send check or money order plus two dollars for postage and handling [Texas residents please add 8.75% sales tax] to
Slough Press, 3009 Normand, College Station, Texas 77845

on **Charles Potts**

Charlie was carrying some luminous poems that night at Shakespeare's—
John Oliver Simon, *Poetry Flash*

A skilled fire-bellied polemicist who happens to share a body with a lyric poet of uncommon gifts—**klipschutz**, *Raven Chronicles*

These **Nature Lovers** poems are like oecologist *Abhorrences*. Ed Dorn salutes you from his grave—**Dennis Formento**, Surregional Press

The same triumphant sense of being a classic outsider—
Hugh Fox, *Home Planet News*

Unparalleled hyperbole and Swiftian wit—**Lee Harris**

Spongebob Square Pants got nothing on him—**Gerald Yelle**, *The Temple*

Charles Potts is the Johnny appleseed of modern Poerty—
Philip Wagner, *The Iconoclast*

Always a good read—**Charles Plymell**, *Zzzzyne* #xxiv

By the time I was finished I was pleasantly surprised and thoroughly satisfied—**Daniel Crocker**, *Chiron Review*

He has meditated extensively on our method of operation and finds the asteroid solution might just be best—**Amalio Madueño**

One thing that stands out in Potts' **Nature Lovers** is the richness of interconnection from poem to poem ... Potts' style is simple in expression but complex in effect. But it is not always in building toward a punch line that his organization resembles a comedian, Potts moves in freedom from bits of anecdote to historical fact to abstract ideas to diatribe to wide open metaphor to call to arms, switching subjects as well as devices within poems in ways that almost seem random except that together they illustrate toward some truth, some truth that need not be said in a tidy way. —**Janice Faye Fiering**, *thetimegarden.com*

The public poetry of Charles Potts leans heavily ... as if the earth itself might shift beneath the dais ... It is one of the longest running odd-man-out acts in American poetry ... he is an outback poet, never a smoothie at one with the in-crowd ... when push comes to shove, Potts eats with the croc's ... He reconfigures the eviscerated Fear Possum by scarring lividity back onto the rot of complacency.—**Ralph LaCharity**, *W'orcs Aloud Allowed*

Charles Potts

Charles Potts was born in Idaho Falls, Idaho, in 1943. He received a BA from Idaho State University in Pocatello, Idaho, in 1965, and received the College of Arts and Sciences at ISU's Distinguished Professional Achievement Award in 1994. He has been publishing and writing since 1963. In 1991 he received Manuscripts International's Creative Excellence in Fiction Award for the novel, *Loading Las Vegas*. He has been a resident of Walla Walla, Washington, since 1978 where he produces the Walla Walla Poetry Party. He is currently the founder of Tsunami Inc., which publishes first edition books of poetry and for five years, *The Temple*, a quarterly of new poetry with contemporary Chinese and Spanish poems with translations. His biography is of record in *Who's Who in the World* and other Marquis publications. *Across the North Pacific* is his twenty-third book.

Smokey Farris

Smokey Farris was born in Dallas, Texas, in 1976. At the age of 12 He met Dirk Michener while attending Fort Worth Christian School and at that time Business Deal Entertainment was born. Business Deal is an artists collective which creates video, recorded music, visual and written arts. Smokey Farris stepped down from his post as Chief of Operations for Business Deal and soon joined Business Deal's Special Projects Division. Travis Catsull and Smokey Farris were able to materialize one such special project with the support of Charles Potts, the food service installation piece, Club Minivan. Smokey was called to duty from a lush artist's life in Austin, Texas to the great northwestern desert to establish Club Minivan with Potts and Catsull. After the fall of Club Minivan, he remained in Walla Walla to serve as Graphic Artist for Tsunami Inc.